From Swamp Yankee to Desert Rat

A Hodgepodge Memoir

By

Peter M. Pegnam

Copyright © 2011 by Peter M. Pegnam

To order additional copies of this book,
visit www.lulu.com

ISBN-978-1-4583-9228-2

Introduction-Preface-Foreword

(Rolled into one. Couldn't figure out the difference)

My wife, Janet, see, goes to some afternoon memoir writing class at the activity center in this here planned community where we now live.

What does she get out of this higher education? She comes home and tells me that I need to write *my* memoirs.

I can only be thankful she didn't sign up for a class on triathlon training, or advanced calculus, or, say, conversational Latin.

In comparison, memoir writing seemed comfortable and I actually started thinking about it. Sometimes, though, I found myself wondering: Why couldn't she have taken a class in the art and science of frying and eating onion rings?

The main obstacle I faced in writing my memoirs, as I saw it, was that I hadn't done anything memoir-worthy. I collected one trophy in my life and that has a small pig on it from a south Tucson eatery with an inscription announcing First Place in Micha's Chimichanga Eating Contest.

I never won the lottery, although I did win a three-speed English bicycle when I was about 12, but only because my mother coordinated an entry box stuffing campaign. It would have been considered an upset if my name had not been drawn from the hundreds of entries.

I did get elevated to president of my high school radio club, but only because the one other kid in the organization didn't want the responsibility. As punishment, I made him vice president.

My foreign adventures thus far have been limited to Canada, a Caribbean cruise and Mexico, where Janet convinced me once during a Mayan pyramid tour in the jungle outside Cancun to cover up lest I get eaten alive by disease-carrying mosquitoes. Thus I became the only tourist out of the thousands there that oppressively sweltering day to be dressed in a heavy, long-sleeve shirt, baggy pants and laced-up shoes with thick socks.

The others – dressed more sensibly in shorts, t-shirts and flip-flops – gave me strange looks and a lot of room.

Try filling up a book with that stuff.

If I were to do a memoir, I reasoned, I would have to ditch the Big Picture concept and start thinking small. That's easy for me. I plunged ahead in no particular order of life, writing things down. Little incidents. As I thought of one, I was reminded of another. I started enjoying myself. Well, I thought, no one else might ever read this but so what? I'm having a good time.

I think I have always been blessed with a sense of humor about most things. Not that I find painful things funny when they are happening, but later, after some of the hurt and embarrassment have worn off.

That spirit is what I found myself trying to capture.

When I found myself struggling to write about something, I chucked it. If I didn't enjoy writing it, I reasoned, who could possibly enjoy reading it?

The only advice I got on memoir writing that I took to heart was to be honest. So, when faced with a topic or event on which I might want to fudge, I had an easy solution: Leave it out.

What I ended up with was not anything resembling a life

history. Just some memories of things that I felt like re-telling for my enjoyment, if no one else's. Nothing more. Nothing less.

Peter Marshall Pegnam

Florence, Arizona

AD 2011

Swamp Yankee

They comprised the famous love triangle in "The Court-ship of Miles Standish" by Henry Wadsworth Longfellow.

John Alden, Priscilla Mullins, Miles Standish: Real people and passengers on the Mayflower's historic voyage to the New World.

I am a descendant of all three. Here's how:

John and Priscilla begot Sarah Alden. Miles, the losing suitor, and his wife, Barbara, begot Alexander Standish.

Sarah and Alexander merged the two family lines by marrying and then producing children, one of whom was Ebenezer Standish.

Ebenezer is my great-great-great-great-great-great-great grandfather. John, Priscilla and Miles go back, of course, two more generations.

This blood line ran through my mother, who grew up in Hanson, Mass., not too far from the original Plymouth Colony.

I was born April 4, 1944 at South County (RI) Hospital, which is just down the road apiece from the Great Swamp Fight locale. That was a terribly bloody 1675 encounter, part of King Philip's War, between the settlers and the Nar-ragansett tribe.

My parents brought me home from South County Hospit-al to the Naval Housing Project in Wickford, RI. My first three years were spent at 13 Greene Street before my parents moved my two brothers and me to another unit in the project at 42 Roosevelt Avenue.

I grew up playing in the fields around the project and walking along the dirt roads that meandered out to the salt water coves and tidal pools of Wickford and through the briar patches and thick woods. (I call these roads, but must say I never saw any cars. The only vehicle I ever did see on any of them was a fire truck that came to douse a grass fire.)

One of these dirt roads sliced between a muddy cove and a stand of poison sumac before skirting a dank briar patch and leading eventually to a grove of trees outside what is now known as Smith's Castle, built in the 1600s.

Everyone I knew growing up always called it Cocumcussoc. I never could pronounce it, but discovered that if you said it real fast, no one seemed to notice.

It was considered a castle by the early settlers because of its heavy fortifications to protect against Indian raids.

It was from here that forces deployed to wage the Great Swamp Fight. Whenever I was out exploring, I imagined them leaving Cocumcussoc and marching to battle along that very same dirt road.

It makes me mighty proud to know that I am descended from the first Pilgrims, that I was born in Great Swamp territory and that I grew up in the shadows, practically, of Smith's Castle at Cocumcussoc.

Picking a Best Friend

Don't you think that you should be able to say who your best friend is without getting into trouble?

Take it from me, that "best friend" question can have its complications.

I was sitting at my desk in Sister Christina's second grade in the basement of St. Bernard's old church hall when a mimeographed piece of paper appeared in front of me. It seemed to be a test of some kind with two blanks to be filled in. It read:

My best friend is _____ because he _____ me.

I wish all quizzes were that easy. Piece of cake. My brother Rich, older than me by four years, was easily my best friend. He was always there, whether to play with me or fight for me. He even walked the long way around to his school so he could accompany me to mine, making sure I got there safely.

I filled in the blanks: My best friend is *Rich* because he *plays with* me.

Sister Christina made the rounds, picking up the completed assignments in order. She placed them in a neat pile on her desk, took the top one and read aloud. It was Mary Alice's, who sat in the front row, left side.

"My best friend is *Jesus* because he *loves* me."

I guess I was a cynic of sorts even at that tender age. I

9

snickered to myself at such a self-serving answer. Just trying to score points with the nun.

Sister Christina said, predictably: "Very good, Mary Alice," and reached for the second one in the stack, from Billy, who sat behind Mary Alice.

"My best friend is *Jesus* because he *loves* me."

Oh, ohh, I thought, Billy's in trouble now. He obviously copied from Mary Alice. This could be bad. Sister Christina was one of the nice nuns, but she had rules. She placed some green tape one day over the mouths of a handful of pupils who talked out loud in class. (Of course, that was nothing compared to the punishments inflicted by Sister Philomena, the Mean One, who adhered strictly to the old rule: Spare the rod and spoil the child.)

To my amazement, Sister Christina smiled and said: "*Very* good, Billy." It was the same with the next pupil and the next. Didn't she see what was going on here? How naive.

She came to the paper filled in by the front row pupil in the second aisle. Same thing:

"My best friend is *Jesus* because he *loves* me."

And the next: "My best friend is *Jesus* because he *loves* me."

It was then that I got the sickening feeling I had missed something or other about this question. Everyone seemed to be exchanging happy, knowing glances as it became apparent to them that they all answered the question correctly.

I was in the back row in the next-to-last aisle, so had to endure a long, agonizing wait for my test paper to reach the top of the pile. I felt like crawling under my desk. In the time I had to wait, I figured that I must have day-dreamed my way through a religion lesson.

The dreaded moment arrived.

"My best friend is *RICH?!*" There was a pause of amazement and then: "Because he *PLAYS WITH* me??!!"

"Peter! Who is Rich?!"

Oh, the laughter of my dear classmates.

Many years later, I was somehow reminded of the incident and told Rich about it. He loved the story and often repeated it.

He didn't seem to mind that when all the second grade votes had been tallied on that day long ago, he came in second – a distant second.

The Eskimo Diet

Mom always urged my brothers and me to eat the fat on our meat. It eventually would serve us well, she insisted. And, in my case anyway, she was right on.

This was more subtle than the standard so-called "food fibs" that parents have long used to entice their young-uns to eat something that their instincts tell them to avoid.

For instance, when the breakfast toast was burnt, Mom would fall back on two strategies to convince us kids to eat the blackened offering. "Burnt toast will make your cheeks rosy" was often the first try. If that didn't work, "burnt toast is better tasting" would follow.

Being the youngest and, therefore the most gullible, I ate a lot of burnt toast.

She also said, and I have come to agree with this, that the end piece of the loaf – the crust – was the best. I guess any morning that the crust was burnt was my lucky day.

She told us the bruises were the best-tasting part of an apple. So guess who would pick the most-bruised apple out of the bowl? Not Mom.

Same with bananas.

Of course, I fell for the carrot and night-vision routine. And to this day I avoid swallowing a watermelon seed. It probably won't sprout a watermelon in my stomach, but why take a chance?

The one thing I really desired was chocolate. But who wanted pimples?

The fatty meat thing would come up at supper. That was our evening meal, by the way, "dinner" being reserved for the mid-day Sunday repast.

As Dad was chewing away on a lean, I am sure, piece of meat, we kids would be fighting for the ones with the biggest globs of fat. And, boy, were they good. You hardly have to chew those suckers at all. They just kinda slide right down. Lips stay moist a long time, too.

Why would we do this?

"If you eat the fat," Mom said countless times, "you'll be able to go out in the winter without your coat on."

To a kid growing up in New England, this seemed a worthy goal.

And it turns out that Mom was right.

But how did she know way back then that I was going to end up living and working and raising a family in southern Arizona?

I guess mothers just know those things.

Project Dwellers

I was probably about 11 that summer day when the local parish Catholic priest came looking for me at the housing project where I lived.

Not to worry. I hadn't done anything wrong – that he knew about anyway.

It seemed that he had promised to play his CYO (Catholic Youth Organization) baseball team against another youth team in a nearby city. His problem was that he didn't own a team. Never had. And game time was just an hour away.

That's why he came to the project. He knew where to find kids, lots of them on short notice, doing what they did most every summer day – playing baseball in a dusty field.

It didn't concern him that I was the only Catholic in the bunch. He needed a team. When there were enough kids who said they had permission to go, off we went.

We showed up for the game with our old gloves, worn shirts, faded dungarees (pant legs rolled up just above the sneakers). We found our opponent was an actual team – complete with crisp uniforms, matching caps and real baseball socks and spikes even. They had a coach. We had a priest.

We played the game on a regulation field, with dugouts. Their pitcher didn't toss the ball toward home plate as we were used to. He threw – hard. We used their baseballs and bats because they weren't held together by tape as were ours.

I wish I could say we showed those city slickers how to play ball. But we didn't.

I can't imagine growing up in a better place than the housing project the Navy threw up in Wickford, RI., near the start of World War II. There were always kids to play with and things to do, outside. I bet most of the kids I grew up with felt the same way. I'm positive the parents didn't care for it at all.

My Mom and Dad moved there with my two older brothers (I hadn't come along yet) in 1941 after Dad was hired as an airplane mechanic at Quonset Point Naval Air Station. A 1957 map I have shows 64 buildings at the housing project. So, 64 x 4 family units per building = a lot of kids.

There were always kids around for that pick-up game of football or baseball and, on occasion, basketball and once, even, a big rock fight. The parents got together to scrape out a ball field in the meadow that adjoined the project. They even built a backstop.

They cleared out a small patch of weeds in another area and stuck up a pole with a basket. It was hard dribbling on dirt, so basketball took a backseat to baseball and football.

When we weren't playing regular sports, there was always tag, or hide-and-seek, or marbles or paying Georgie Blake to eat a caterpillar, things like that. This is what made the project fun, for a kid.

The parents had to endure tight quarters and constant noise and virtually no privacy. The walls were paper thin.

Downstairs we had a small kitchen and living room. The kitchen was so small that we had to slide the table up against the wall when not in use. When it was pulled out, there was no room to get through.

In one corner, my mother kept the clothes washing machine, pulling it out and hooking it up to the sink when it was in use.

It was old and had a wringer. The clothes were hung outside to dry and, in the winter, to freeze. She used starch for whites, which then needed ironing.

Every so often the washing machine would break and Mom thought her prayers had been answered and she'd get a newer version. Much to her frustration, Dad would always repair it and get it back into service. After all, he was an aircraft mechanic.

The project had a recreation hall that served as a kindergarten and hosted Boy Scout meetings. Dad was a Boy Scout leader for a while.

A big Boy Scout jamboree was held one year in a large field at the end of our street. I have pictures of me outside my brother Bob's tent. I was five years old and jealous.

It was on this occasion that Dad had to pick up Chief Adams of the Narragansett tribe. He brought the wrinkled man to our place to wait until it was time to go the encampment. The chief taught me to beat the war drum. I still remember how.

Another character at the show was a fellow whose pitch was: "Shake the hand that shook the hand of Buffalo Bill." He had a long line of Scouts waiting to do so.

My father had been a professional roller skater in his youth. He and his partner had a Vaudeville act. He kept a wooden roller skating mat rolled up in our basement. Every so often, he would take the mat over to the recreation hall and do a little act.

On one of these occasions, he held me face down and by the ankles as he spun around and around in a tight circle. I had a kitchen match clenched between my teeth.

He spun me lower and lower until the match touched the mat and ignited. I was in show business and loved it.

But I had higher ambitions. When asked the inevitable: What do you want to be when you grow up?, I would answer, to my parents' horror, "A coal man."

These were the guys that loaded up our coal bins. They'd fill a large sack with coal from their truck and haul it over to the bin and dump it in. Their hands and faces were black from the dust. I couldn't wait until I was big enough.

There were other guys who really disgusted my mother. They pumped the cesspools. There were two things mom couldn't stand. One was that, when Nature called, they urinated against their truck tire. The other was that when it was time to eat lunch they would sit on the big hose running from the cesspool to their truck and chow down. The hose would be throbbing from the pumping action and they would just bounce up and down, chewing away.

The Whiting Company delivered milk door-to-door. It was kept chilled in the truck with chunks of ice. Sometimes on a hot day we would try to swipe a small piece of ice without the milkman seeing and yelling at us.

The ice cream truck came regularly in the summer. One lucky year, the man who drove the truck lived on our street, just a few doors down from us. Once in a while, not too often, he'd give away a few Popsicles at the end of his day.

Crime and (Escaping) Punishment

The Village of Wickford was established in 1709 and contains an astounding collection of Colonial homes on tree-lined, waterfront streets. Postcard scenery.

In the middle of this, in all its wisdom, is where the Navy built a housing project for the civilians being added to its rapidly growing workforce at Quonset Point in the build-up to World War II.

The project, not attractive by any definition, looked like a military base. Rows of long, stark two-story structures with four units apiece. They had white shingles (asbestos?) on the exterior walls and coal bins jutting out onto barren front yards. The cramped backyards were dominated by clotheslines.

The locals were not happy with this ugly government project, or these newcomers.

When rationing came, my mother would take her meat stamps and walk to Ryan's Market, where the butcher would tell her they had no meat. One day, after hearing this yet again, she left the store in tears. A local woman outside asked her what was wrong.

She took my mother's rationing stamps and cash, marched inside and bought the meat for my mother. The store had meat, but not for the project dwellers.

This kindly lady made arrangements to purchase meat for

my mom thereafter.

The town didn't want to open its schools to the project kids but couldn't find a way around it. They did find, though, that they were not required to provide school buses for the project, and they didn't.

One day, an unexpected fierce rain storm erupted just as my Catholic elementary school was getting out. There was general mayhem as everyone was running for the buses. I thought I'd give it a try and headed for bus No. 2, the one I knew drove right past the project. I dove in, ducked my head down and rushed by the driver and made it unnoticed, I thought.

After everyone was on and seated, the driver got up and came to my seat and escorted me off the bus.

I was thoroughly drenched after just a few steps. I was alone, as most the other kids my age from the project attended the elementary public school in another part of town. I went to St. Bernard's, learning academics and discipline from the Sisters of the Cross and Passion. On my lonely walk home, which was about a mile in length, I passed by the baseball and football playing fields of the public high school.

The high school had recently planted a very long row of tiny hedge plants between the fields and the road. They were planted neatly in freshly turned earth, which by the time I got there that day had turned to mud.

Well, I couldn't get into any worse condition, I reasoned. So, as any normal boy would, I decided to walk in the mud. As I did so, I stepped on a tiny hedge plant and it snapped. Down into the muck it went. A goner. An accident? I don't remember.

What I do remember is continuing on, as if in a trance, stepping on and snapping every single hedge plant. It was a long row, perhaps 200 yards. Got every one, I think. Once you start, it's hard to stop.

My mother, appalled at my miserable condition when I got home, queried me about my mud encrusted shoes ("I accidentally stepped in a mud puddle"), and ordered me to take off my wet clothes and get into a hot tub.

Over night it turned cold. On my walk to school the next morning, as I passed by the crime scene, I discovered much to my horror that my footprints had been frozen into place.

I suddenly felt as if every occupant of every car going by were looking at my shoes and saying: "He's the one! He did it!"

I made it through the next couple of days without being taken into custody, but a complication presented itself Sunday morning.

I had to go to Mass with my parents. They parked in the lot across the street from the church. This meant we had to walk across the street and, as usual, a Rhode Island State Trooper was on hand to get pedestrians safely across.

I only had the one pair of shoes, so naturally I had them on. I got on the side of my parents farthest from the Trooper and tried to walk in tandem so the officer might not spot The Shoes.

Expecting to hear a "Stop! Police!" command at any moment, I was scared to death. I made it, but no sooner had I gotten into the asylum of the church that I realized I would have to run the gauntlet again after Mass.

This went on for weeks until slowly I felt I had gotten away with it. For whatever reason, the high school never again planted hedges along the road.

As long as we're on the subject of the project and wrong-doing, I might as well confess to another incident that occurred a few years before.

The older boys (ages 10-11 maybe), were taking a break from their football game when one of them called the others over to a wall of the project's recreation building. He pointed at something on the wall and everyone started hooting and giggling and then laughing hysterically.

When they went back to playing football, I sauntered over to the wall to see what the commotion was all about. There in very, very tiny letters written lightly in pencil were four letters: fuck.

I had no idea what that might mean or why it was so attention-grabbing, but after the game was over and everyone had left, I got to work.

There were a few roofing shingles that had blown down onto the ground and I bent these back and forth a couple of times to make a crack and reveal a dark, tarry substance inside. Using these as an artist might wield a giant brush I wrote in letters, as big as a small child could, FUCK.

There, I thought, if those letters were funny small, wait until they see them big. It should be hilarious.

I was there the next day when the older boys arrived for their game. I was surprised at their reaction. They didn't find it funny at all. They were shocked. It was if they felt they would all share in some kind of blame. Who, they said, would have done such a terrible thing?

Hmmm, I thought. Maybe that's not a funny word after all. Maybe, I said to myself, I should keep quiet about this. Some of the parents did see this graffiti and they were upset and speculated out loud what kind of juvenile delinquent might have done such a terrible thing. No one suspected such a small, innocent lad such as myself.

In spite of what the townspeople thought, the project was filled with good people. One man across the street from us had a leading role in the development of the Quonset Hut. Up the street a little ways was the man who formed the town's first Little League.

Sometime around 1956, the Navy set a deadline for all the civilian families to be out of the project. They were easing in more and more Navy personnel and needed the space for them.

We moved to a house on Pleasant Street in Wickford's historic district, where I developed more good memories. I was nostalgic about the project though and missed it after we moved.

Within 20 years, Quonset Point was decommissioned and the project demolished. Today it's called Wilson Park and filled with formal ball fields.

The town finally got its wish.

Many years later, I was reading a newspaper article about ⌐rd. One long-time local woman referenced the project by calling it simply "what the Navy inflicted on us."

I'd like to think she meant the buildings; not the people.

Avoiding Taxes – Legally

Seldom, if ever, do you get a chance as a kid to outwit a grown-up and beat the system at the same time. I still savor my long-ago moment.

In possession of 30 cents, I was in Earnshaw's Rexall Drug in downtown Wickford to do some serious buying.

Normally with that kind of money my shopping decisions would have to do with whether to buy the 5-cent candy bars (quantity) or the 10-cent ones (quality), or a combination. I might even decide to throw in a 10-cent comic book.

I don't recall why this particular day I had come to buy only comic books. Perhaps I still had a candy stash left from Halloween.

What I do recall is taking my three carefully chosen comic books to the lady at the cash register, at the end of the soda fountain, and placing my quarter and nickel on the counter.

To my surprise and chagrin, she informed me I needed 31 cents. She patiently explained at great length about something called a sales tax. This had never happened to me before. Maybe it was new or maybe the other clerks just let it go. This one, however, told me how if I spent a dollar, the grand total would be $1.04. A 50-cent sale would become 52 cents and a 25-cent sale would be 26 cents.

So, she informed me, you'll have to come up with another

penny, which I did not have, or put one of the comic books back. She asked: "Do you understand?" Her explanation had been so thorough that I actually understood very well, I thought. So I put my theory to the test.

I slid one comic book off the counter and held it by my side. I pushed my quarter toward her to pay for the remaining two. She smiled and gave me my change. One nickel. There was no tax on 20 cents. Thanks to her detailed explanation, I had figured correctly.

I took her nickel and put it back on the counter with my nickel and put the third comic book back down. "Now," I said, "I'll take this one."

The clerk frowned and grumbled, reluctantly selling me my third comic book. Gracious in victory, I said nothing and maintained my best poker face. My insides, though, had a wide grin. I had beaten the grown-ups at their own game!

The Art of Giving

The most memorable Christmas present I ever got was a jar of peanut butter that didn't have any peanut butter in it.

It was back when Christmas was pretty much the same as it is today: an ordeal, to be survived so as to make it through to the best day of the year. And that would be the glorious Day After Christmas, when people of all ages finally relax and play with their toys.

The ordeal that year started with Midnight Mass. To a young lad, who would rather be in bed, this seemed punishing. And not just any Mass was this. After all, if you are going to drag your faithful out of their pajamas and warm living rooms on a cold winter night, why not give them the full treatment?

That of course meant High Mass. Translation: Really, really long, and a trifle smoky from the extra candles and incense.

Christmas morning meant getting all dressed up again. No, not for another church service but for something even more important: The trip to my Pegnam grandparents in Brockton, Mass., (the hometown, by the way, of heavyweight boxing champ Rocky Marciano).

This meant two hours in a stuffy 1937 Plymouth to cover the 60 miles of two-lane roads.

My father was the eldest of five. Everyone of the five had

at least two children and everyone came. Presents were exchanged, good food was had. But if a psychologist did a word association thing on those annual gatherings, the best description, I think, would be "chaotic."

Eventually, always after dark, we would leave and drive a few miles over to the small town of Hanson (which was, incidentally, the original hometown of the Ocean Spray Cranberry Company). That's where my mother's relatives gathered. That meant we could take off our neckties, unbutton the shirt collars and get comfortable.

Their abodes were more humble than the Pegnam one. Instead of a present exchange, there was a grab bag, which consisted of a pillowcase. Instead of a formal dinner there were simple desserts and hot coffee lightened with milk right out of the can.

Everyone would toss a gift-wrapped offering into the pillowcase. There was always a limit on what a gift could cost. It wasn't much.

Not everyone tossed in a gender-neutral package. A pair of nylons made it into the bag one year and drawn, of course, by a guy. Trading would commence as soon as everyone had opened a gift.

This is how I ended up with a jar labeled PEANUT BUTTER:

My Aunt Esther was behind it, if memory serves. I think everyone else was in on it.

Seems as if I was the last one to draw, when there was just one package left.

The package to my relief was of a size that I felt sure could not contain nylons.

Tearing off the paper, I stared dejectedly at the PEANUT BUTTER jar. Everyone can tell when a kid is crestfallen and I sure was. Not only was this a crummy jar of peanut butter but I was deathly allergic to peanuts.

Aunt Esther told me that this was made from a different kind of peanuts. This I could eat, she assured me. Open it up and smell it, she said.

With everyone watching, I fell for it.

Just as I got the lid loosened enough, a coiled up green spring erupted toward my face. A loud round of laughter also erupted from everyone in the room.

I had been had but good.

I didn't try to trade that gift. I kept it for many years. Every so often I would loosen the lid and, pointing it away from my face, let the coiled up snake fly into the air.

At those moments, alone in my room, I could almost see those laughing red faces again and hear the roars and feel the warmth.

Supply and Demand

Fiddler crabs are marvelous little creatures. They are only an inch or two across. The males possess a big claw that female fiddler crabs find attractive. It says so in the books.

Growing up in Wickford and splashing around in the mud during low tide on a summer day teaches a lad three things about fiddler crabs.

One is that fiddler crabs are quick and can disappear down their little holes in the blink of an eye.

Two is that they don't go down very deep into their holes. So a young boy armed with a stick can sink it into the mud effectively blocking the crab from going any deeper. Prying the stick up pops the crab out of its hole.

Three is that the fiddler crab claw is not just a sexual adornment. It can pinch. Hard. And draw blood from a small finger.

There was a bait store in Wickford that sold fiddler crabs.

The proprietor told me and my business partner, who at age 13 was older than I and thus in charge, that he would gladly buy fiddler crabs from us for 50 cents a quart.

Fifty cents in the mid-1950s. We're talking big bucks here.

We got into his small skiff and rowed over at low tide to Cornelius Island. There was a little cove there that was just loaded with fiddlers.

We set about with our bucket and sticks and nabbed quite a few. We got pretty good at picking them up by the big claw without getting nipped but a couple of times.

It was back-breaking work, chasing after the crabs in the slippery mud and bending over and all. When we tired of it, we took our haul to the bait shop, where the owner carefully measured our crabs and paid us as agreed. If memory serves, I think my partner and I split about 80 cents.

It takes a lot of fiddlers to make a quart, we learned.

I told my parents about our new business. They smiled. My friend told his grandfather, who had a lobster boat and knew a thing or two about fiddler crabs. He smiled in a knowing sort of way. But he didn't let on.

We continued with our enterprise for several days. But our enthusiasm was waning. It was then that Grandfather Lobsterman, let us in on a little secret.

Dig a hole on the beach, says he, and sink your bucket into it up to the rim. Put some remnants of dead fish in the bottom of the bucket for bait. Then go sit in the shade for a couple of hours. Come back and you'll have a bucket full of fiddlers. They get in. Can't get out. Ingenious.

We did as he said and it worked. We were rich! Rich beyond imagination! We were absolutely giddy as we toted our haul to the bait shop.

The proprietor was stunned. He was truly sorry, he explained, but there was no way he could sell so many fiddler crabs. He was nice about it and bought what he could use. About a quart.

Not surprisingly, he stayed in business many years. My friend and I dissolved our partnership that very day.

Supply and demand.

Ornithology

I wish I knew when my bird attack happened. It had to be right around 1963, which was the year Alfred Hitchcock's movie "The Birds" was released. Just coincidence. Here's my real-life nightmare:

I started by using pieces of stale white bread on that mis-leadingly calm summer day to snare an ample supply of bait in our minnow trap. My plan was to catch a few flounder for the evening meal.

I pointed our family skiff out beyond the breakwater to a spot I had fished before, not too far the the old lighthouse. My only companion was our dog Bill.

I anchored, baited my hook and dropped my line almost to the bottom, where the delicious flatfish were known to hang out. All was peaceful.

That's when the first wave of attackers struck, out of nowhere.

I heard a screech and looked up to see a tern heading straight for my face. It seemed possessed. Its beak was wide open, talons in full attack mode, a look of sheer evil in its beady eyes. And that scream!

I ducked as it peeled away at the last moment. Then the second one came. And another. It was then I noticed that the beasts had formed a circle in the sky and were in forma-tion, taking turns at dive-bombing and trying to make some kind of a point. Very effectively, I might add.

I noticed that Bill was taking his share of abuse as well. He ducked the first few attackers, but then sought shelter under a seat. I couldn't fit.

I had to fight it out. I used an oar to fend off a few attackers, but I saw that fresh troops were being pressed into action and the battle intensified.

I heard an interior bugle sound "retreat," so, waving my trusty oar, made my way to the bow and started to pull anchor. That's when two complications arose.

It takes two arms to pull up an anchor effectively. I needed to keep one free for fighting. And when I did lift the anchor a little, the boat was blown in the direction of the menacing rocks encircling the lighthouse.

As I saw it, I needed two arms for pulling up the anchor, one arm for fighting and one arm for using a second oar to keep the boat off the rocks, which were menacingly close. I believe the terns sensed my predicament and stepped up their assault.

In the interest of brevity, let me say that by some miracle I eventually got my outboard motor started and was able to drag anchor enough to escape.

I had been to this location many times before and had never been attacked. Once even, after realizing we had caught too many scup, my brother and I tossed the extras up onto the lighthouse for the terns, and they seemed appreciative for the handout.

I figured that this time it was probably nesting season and the terns were protecting their young on the lighthouse grasses. Whatever the reason, I gave the lighthouse wide berth thereafter.

Terns are often described as seagulls on a smaller scale. I actually thought I had a pet seagull for a while, but it wasn't true.

It was during my quahogging career. Whenever I sat down to eat lunch, a seagull would appear as if by magic and take up position beside my boat. I'd toss him some scraps. I knew it was always the same one because of this red spot on its beak.

I later learned that all seagulls have this red spot.

There are two other seagull stories from my youth that I shouldn't tell, but...

We had a friend who delighted in fishing for gulls, a protected species. He would bait his hook with a fish and then place it out on a dock or on the deck of an unoccupied boat. He would hide under a pier just in case a fish warden might pass by. When the gull took the bait and the hook and headed skyward, the fight was on.

His pole would be bent to near breaking as he reeled the gull in from the sky. A violent, ugly sport and I mention it only as a comparison to my more gentle pastime.

This wasn't my idea, but I tried it out a couple of times. Please do not repeat this experiment.

I tied one end of a fishing line to a piece of eel and then tied the other end of the line to a second piece of eel. The line was perhaps 100 feet long. I placed each end out where a passing gull might see it.

Before long, a gull would see one piece of eel and swallow it. He would take off, unsuspectingly, with the other piece of eel swinging in the air, dangling at the end of the line. Ho-ho-ho. Another gull would see that piece of eel flying through the air and catch it and swallow it in mid-air. So, we've got two flying seagulls, see, with a piece of fishing line running between them.

As the gulls flew apart, one of them would jerk the eel from the other's belly. So that gull would see the eel that had just been pulled from his gut flying through the air and go get it and then the other gull …

Well, you get the picture. You had to be there, and I'm kind of sorry I was.

The Big Leagues

The corporal punishment administered freely by the Sisters of the Cross and Passion at St. Bernard's was minor league stuff.

The Christian Brothers at La Salle Academy in Providence, R.I., represented the big leagues.

Our sophomore English teacher, for example, sent us to the school library one day during class so everyone could fetch a book to read and to write a report on. When we returned, he lined us up around the room for a book inspection. One of my fine Italian friends, Sal, had chosen a volume that didn't have many pages but did, unfortunately for him, have a hard cover.

The Brother suspected Sal had chosen the thinnest book he could find and asked him: "What's this?" Replied Sal in a Rocky Balboa type tone: "Hey. Itza good book."

The good Brother slammed the corner of the book into Sal's face, leaving an ugly welt outside and a severe split inside his mouth. Blood spilled from the wound, which angered the kind Brother even more. He kicked Sal out of class and told him not to return until he quit bleeding.

When my brother Rich was introduced to La Salle, a Christian Brother was explaining that for every hour spent in class, students were expected to spend two hours doing homework. Rich did some quick mental arithmetic. There were six classes a day, which meant 12 hours of homework.

Add to that the time spent commuting and Rich had a simple question: "When do we sleep?"

Just to make sure he had heard correctly, the Brother had him repeat the question before pounding him in the side of the head for insolence.

It was also during my sophomore year that it was known that one Brother had it in for a certain senior athlete. One day, just a few weeks shy of graduation, there was an encounter in a hallway. Words were exchanged and then punches.

The Brother, a large man but old and overweight, was no match for the young athlete and ended up a bloody mess on the floor. The student was promptly expelled. I suspect he never regretted it.

La Salle was an all-boy school with a student body of 1,300. As such, it had a lot of fine athletes to draw from for its teams. But even that wasn't good enough. Parish priests throughout the state were expected to keep an eye out for exceptional athletes and convince the parents to send them to La Salle.

If more convincing were needed, the priest could make arrangements to help with the small monthly tuition and the cost of textbooks. If the family wasn't Catholic, it didn't matter.

My brother, an excellent baseball player, tried out for the La Salle team. He never had a chance. The coach had his team all set, from among the "scholarship" players he was expected to play.

This state-wide recruiting produced some exceptional teams. The hockey players, mostly students from the

French-speaking areas of northern Rhode Island, sharpened their skills with pre-season games against Providence College and Brown University squads.

La Salle even had a rifle team, which was trained by the Reserve Officer Training Corps sergeant at Providence College. They competed against, among others, West Point.

The cross country team had never come close to losing the New England Catholic championship race.

There was a strict smoking policy at La Salle in those years. Smoking was prohibited outside and inside, except in the Smoking Room, which was in the basement. And freshmen were not allowed into the Smoking Room.

To smoke at La Salle Academy, you see, you had to be 15 years old and a sophomore.

Students were required to wear jackets and ties. If you showed up without a tie, you had to rent one from the office. Those ties shared one quality. They were all hideous.

Although there is a Christian Brother brandy made, our guys were beer drinkers. A large beer truck made regular deliveries to the brick building that housed the Brothers. The driver would roll a dolly loaded with cases of beer down the truck's ramp and into the rear of the building. He made a lot of trips up and down the ramp.

We used to joke that you could tell how long someone had been a Brother by the girth of his belly.

La Salle separated students according to scholastic ability. The best-achieving freshmen were in Class 1A, for example, sophomores 2A, etc. The further down the alphabet you got, the more you would encounter students who were not as scholastically inclined (to put it as gently as possible).

Thus as you got into 1G or 2F or 3H or whatever, the more likely you were to encounter, let's say, hockey players without front teeth. I started out in 1B, did well, and was then placed in 2A my sophomore year and 3A my junior year. My senior year, because I wanted an unusual combination of classes, I was given the only option available: Something like 4H for my home room.

As part of the senior year, the Brothers would send each class separately to a Catholic-run retreat operated by the Diocese out in the country. It was to be a quiet weekend of prayer and contemplation, two days and two nights.

I apparently slept through all the fun that weekend but learned that it involved nighttime forays and the animals on a neighboring farm. The farmer was very upset. The director of the retreat told us how many years he had been running the operation before honoring us as the worst group he had ever encountered.

A special bus was sent and we were escorted with a guard back to La Salle on Sunday to be threatened with mass expulsion. Nothing ever happened.

La Salle had a grueling schedule. There were six classes, a full schedule, every day. These were real classes, too, with no soft spots: French, Latin, History, English, Calculus and the like filled the day. No study halls or shops. There were report cards every two weeks. My brother, Rich, had been right. Sleep had not been figured into their equation. I sometimes ran track after school and then had to take a city bus to downtown Providence. There I caught the Shore Line bus to Wickford and then walked home. This added up to a 12-hour day – before the homework.

The bi-weekly report cards accounted for 40 percent of the grade. That meant a lot of written tests every day. The big quarterly exams made up the other 60 percent.

There was no way to get all the homework done. I learned to wing it, figuring out which teachers really were going to have a test the next day and which ones wouldn't. I remember this one time guessing wrong with happy results. I had figured the English teacher was bluffing. Between classes, though, I had five minutes to get through the 20 or so pages of text he had assigned.

I had just enough time to read the footnotes. There was a test. But the teacher took every single question from the footnotes. I aced it. Only two other students passed, barely. Everyone else complained loud and bitterly. They had studied.

If you failed one class for the year, you were allowed to come back the next if you made up the class in summer school. Fail two classes and you were out. That's what happened to Rich. He hated school. I think he was relieved to finish up in the more relaxed atmosphere of the public school.

My oldest brother, Bob, graduated eventually, but it was a doubt for a while.

When I went to register at La Salle with my parents in the spring of 1958, we encountered the principal – a large, intimidating figure – in the hallway. When he saw us coming he exclaimed in a booming voice: "Oh, my God. Not another Pegnam!" He wasn't trying to be funny.

On my first day in Latin class, the teacher walked in and said nothing. He peered ominously over his glasses, scanning the assembled students.

Eventually he spoke, in a sneering sort of way: "Where's Pegnam?" I shrunk, silently, in my seat. He raised his voice: "Where's Pegnam?" It sounded threatening. I lifted my hand, slightly. He approached my desk until he was just a few inches away.

My family felt there was some personal animosity between him and our Parish priest, but didn't know what. This same teacher had given Bob a hard time and had flunked Rich.

He stared down at me. "I had your brothers," he said before cackling in a menacing sort of way.

Welcome to La Salle, I said to myself. The Big Leagues.

The Wickford Shellfish

Soon after the first light drifted into my bedroom on the second floor of our house on Pleasant Street, I would hear the first quahog boat of the day heading out from its pier in Wickford Harbor, out into Narragansett Bay, outside the huge boulders that made up the breakwater.

Out past the red and black buoys that marked the channel. Out past the old lighthouse standing watch. Out to where the day's catch might be waiting, somewhere between Jamestown Island and the mainland, some lucky spot, perhaps.

There were other areas the quahoggers couldn't go. Off limits, the state declared. Polluted waters.

As the quahoggers of my youth said, and perhaps they say so still: "A polluted quahog is a dead quahog." They didn't buy in to that government nonsense that said a living quahog was bad to eat because it came from the other side of an imaginary line.

As a result, on some mornings as I lay in bed, I wouldn't hear just one boat and then another and then another going out over time as was usual. I would hear instead a lot of quahog boats leaving in a very short time, and early, too. A roar of outboard motors. An Oklahoma land rush, as it were, on Rhode Island water.

From by bed, when I heard the day start that way, I

would know without opening my eyes what the morning weather had to offer: Fog. Thick and lots of it.

The quahoggers were in a rush because they were "going over the line" to where the government told them they couldn't dig. On this day, in the fog, they couldn't be seen. They wouldn't have much time because the fog would lift. But that was OK because their catch would be double perhaps of what they could get in the legal waters, where there were fewer quahogs.

And in half the time. Maybe less. They had to be gone before the fog.

The quahoggers I came to know were hard-working, far from wealthy, tough, and proud. They didn't just head out to work when the weather was nice. They had families to feed. Sometimes a bigger boat would be needed to break a channel in the ice so they could work the freezing waters on a frigid winter day. On such days they would drink hot coffee from a Thermos and urinate on their hands to ward off frostbite.

Little did I realize as a young boy listening to the quahog boats from the comfort of my bed that one day I would be working at the Wickford Shellfish, where many of the quahoggers kept their boats and sold their catches. I would be weighing their day's take, paying them from the store's cash box, listening to their stories. And loving it.

I came to this wonderful job because of an unfortunate ending to my previous summer employment. I had spent the summer I was 15 working as a dishwasher at the Howard Johnson Restaurant, located at the junction of Routes 1 and 1A in Wickford. It was reputed to be the largest HoJo's in the country.

The following two summers I worked the counter. The shifts were nine hours long, but we got paid for eight as we were, in theory, allowed two 15-minute breaks and 30 minutes for lunch. We got one free meal a day, as long as we ordered something simple off the lunch menu.

There was one time when my brother Bob was the chef and I was washing dishes that I got a wonderful feast. Bob asked me if I wanted Salisbury steak. To that he added a big helping of potatoes, extra gravy, and more odds and ends.

I was being getting fattened up for the slaughter, I discovered. As I was chowing down I learned that he was trying to get rid of all the last remnants of food from the pots and pans so I could get them all scrubbed clean before I left work.

We worked 48 hours a week and got paid for 40. Pay was $1 a hour. A "promotion" to the counter brought some extra money in the form of tips. But not much. We probably weren't the most loyal of workers. Occasionally, someone would ask what I recommended for lunch.

"Do you like seafood?" I would ask. If they replied in the affirmative, I would point to an unassuming open-air eatery across the street and say: "They have really good food." Many people took me up on that recommendation and walked over. Some actually came back after lunch to thank me.

Toward the end of the third summer, I had a brief spat with the manager's wife, who had just emerged from a long spell in the cocktail lounge in an ugly mood. In ceremonious fashion, I undid my apron, wadded it up, handed it to her and, not being original, said simply: "I quit."

That's what brought me the next spring in search of a summer job to the Wickford Shellfish, then located at the water's edge where Esmond and Enfield avenues converge.

I had never entered this place of business before, even though it was within easy walking distance of our home. The store sold fresh fish and lobster that it bought directly from the fishermen. The business was mostly a family affair, I would learn.

I found out that Eddie Archambault was the boss. When I asked him for employment, he told me he had never hired any summer help before, but added, after a pause, that he thought his younger brother, Dick, might appreciate it.

He hired me on the spot, and told me the pay would be $1.50 an hour and to show up for work at 8 a.m. the first day of summer vacation, about two months away. A 50 percent raise!

My parents were suspicious, though. I didn't know why, but their attitude created doubts in my own mind.

So, on occasion, I would drop by the Shellfish to check in with Eddie to see if he remembered me and our deal. He said he did.

On the appointed day, I showed up for my new job to find only Eddie's brother, Dick, around. The retail part of the business was not yet open. Dick took care of the processing end in the back and out on the piers.

I had never met Dick, and he wasn't expecting me. I told him Eddie hired me for the summer. Dick was surprised that Eddie hadn't informed him.

Maybe my parents were right, I thought.

Dick frowned at the sneakers on my feet and found me an old pair of rubber boots to wear. He told me I'd have to buy some boots. But first, he was going to have to talk to his brother about me. He muttered something about not needing any help. I think he was 53 years old.

I eagerly pitched in to help Dick with his early chores, which included some fairly heavy lifting. I think by the time Eddie showed up a couple of hours later, Dick could see the benefit of having a younger back around.

By the time a week passed, I felt like part of the family. My parents were still leery.

The wives of Eddie and Dick, along with George Cutting, handled the retail sales. George, I found out, kept small bottles of gin stashed around the environs. This was widely known, although George thought it was secret. Dick warned me to be careful before moving any crate as I might dislodge one of George's bottles.

One time, Dick told me, he jerked a crate and a gin bottle went flying to the concrete floor and broke. Without thinking, Dick turned to George, who was right there, and said, "Oh. George! I'm sorry!" George disavowed any knowledge of the bottle.

I noticed during this break-in period that Eddie's eyes seemed to get heavy in the afternoon and, I thought, his speech became slightly slurred.

It was on some such afternoon that he asked me how many days I had been working. He said something about his accountant, Mr. Tandy, being out of town and unable to cut a proper paycheck with deductions and all.

I told Eddie I had worked 10 days. He wanted to know

how many hours. Eighty, I replied. How much, he asked, was I promised per hour.

Nervously, the words catching in my throat, I answered, $1.50 an hour. It seemed like so much money. He turned, walked over to the cash register and, swaying back and forth slightly, opened it, took out some bills and came back and presented me with $120.

I couldn't wait to get home and tell my parents.

Fish Market Show Biz

I never considered the fish market business synonymous with the entertainment industry, until I experienced a summer at the Wickford Shellfish.

Eddie, the boss, was famous for his clam chowder, which he made in a huge kettle – the size of the ones you see the head-hunters in cartoon strips use to cook the missionary. On chowder days, Eddie's cocktail hour came early, about breakfast time. This was an all day affair – for both chowder and cocktails.

He was proud of his recipe and stirred it almost constantly with a wooden oar as the broth simmered away. It was a concentrate that was sold in the Shellfish store and shipped frozen across the country.

It smelled so good that on days he was making it folks from the neighborhood would catch a whiff and stop by for a visit – and, they hoped, a sample. Sometimes a small crowd would form. Eddie glowed with pride (and possibly something else). Chowder days were fun.

Eddie's brother, Dick, and their hired hand, George Cutting, were so skilled and fast at fileting fish that folks would gather around them in the back shop on many days to watch them in action. Knives would flash as a stack of fish would be replaced in no time by a large pan of filets and a wastebasket of skeletal remains. There would be murmurs of appreciation from the crowd.

One of my jobs was to keep the salt-water bins out front in the retail section filled with live lobsters that we bought directly from the boats.

Lobsters have two claws: the smaller one, which is the fast-moving pincher and the big, slower one, the crusher. Some of the lobster fishermen would put a stout rubber band around the crusher claw. Others would keep it out of action by inserting a small wooden peg into the claw's joint. They didn't worry about the pincher. And some of the lobstermen did nothing with either claw.

The pincher claw would hurt and draw blood if it got you. But the crusher, if it got a hold, could break a bone. We used to demonstrate this to customers by placing an empty Coke bottle in the crusher claw. The lobster would pulverize it.

When I brought crates of live lobsters into the retail store, I had to reach in to this mass of lobsters, pluck them out and hurl them into their appropriate bins. The lobsters didn't cooperate. They all snuggled in so that only their action-packed front ends were showing.

Also, I had to get each lobster into the right bin. This meant sorting them on the fly into 1¼-pounders, 1½-pounders, 1¾-pounders and culls (missing a claw or two).

It seemed amazing to me that after just a short while I could plainly differentiate the sizes. And being young and sober, even, I eventually could grab them without getting pinched. I did this chore so frequently that I actually got to the point that I could grab two lobsters with each hand and, by using both hands, pretty much keep the air filled with flying lobsters until my crate was empty and all the lobsters had flown into the right bins.

I got so fast that a small crowd of customers would gather round at whatever time I was doing this. I had added my own act to the show.

But there was no question who the star was. Her name was Naomi and she lived nearby.

One of my jobs was to cook lobsters, lots of them in this big steel tank out on the dock. These lobsters were to be cleaned and their meat sold by the pound.

That's where Naomi came in. She would show up on these appointed days with the tools of her trade, which included a large rubber mallet and a variety of picking and cracking instruments.

Regulars would call well in advance wanting to know when Naomi's next performance would be.

Wearing a rubber apron and rubber boots, a costume of sorts, I guess, she would get to work on the stainless steel counters in the backshop. Showtime.

As often as I watched it, I never could believe how quickly this young lady could take a large lobster and separate it into shell remnants on one side and a pile of precious meat on the other. A blur. Too fast to grasp. And that's why the regulars hated to miss a performance.

Just as an aside, some of the lobsters we kept in bins in a shed out over the dock were very big. We saved them for cooking. Tourists walking out on the docks were amazed at their sizes and frequently asked me to hold one up for a picture.

So if you see an old picture of a skinny kid with floppy boots holding up a big lobster on a dock, it could be me.

I loved the Wickford Shellfish, though the work was hard and smelly. More than once a cat or two, drawn by the aroma of fish, followed me on my walk home after work at 5 p.m. My mother made me undress in the back entryway before coming into the house and I had to take a bath before eating.

I used to think: That's no way to treat someone in Show Business.

Long Live the Crab!

I read recently that horseshoe crabs have been around for 250 million years, give or take. The article noted that one reason the crabs have escaped extinction is that they can tolerate extremes in temperatures.

Can I ever vouch for that.

I was working that summer at the Wickford Shellfish. One morning, I spotted a horseshoe crab pushing itself through the shallow waters near the long pier where the quahog boats tied up.

I had, a few days earlier, purchased an eel pot and knew that a chopped up horseshoe crab would make excellent bait for the pot. I waded in and picked up the crab by its long tail. I wouldn't be needing its services for a few days, so I wrapped it up in a burlap sack and placed in on a shelf in the store's large walk-in freezer, which was kept in the zero degree range.

And then I forgot about it.

Two months later, toward the end of summer, I was cleaning out the freezer when I discovered my crab, frozen solid, of course. I took it out of the bag and tossed it into a large wooden keg that we kept as a garbage can outside.

I was busily at work a couple of hours later when I heard a strange scratching noise in the keg. Peering in, I was shocked to see that the sun had thawed out the crab and it was very much alive and trying to get out.

I picked it up by its tail and took it back to the shallow water where I had found it. I set it down, and away it swam. I think horseshoe crabs are going to be around for a v-e-r-y long time.

These creatures technically are not crabs, by the way, but this is not a scientific paper. They have a hard shell topside and are relatively slow moving on land. They grow to about 12-18 inches, with their long, hard spike of a tail extending out a few more inches.

We had a dog that for some reason seemed to harbor a deep hatred for horseshoe crabs.

Bill, that was his name, was part cocker spaniel and part beagle and took to the water. He loved going out with us in our little 14-foot skiff, perched on the prow, ears flapping in the wind, our own, living figurehead.

When we'd stop far out from shore, he couldn't wait to dive in. Sometimes he'd sink a little too deep with this dive and we'd have to reach down, grab him by his collar and tug him up to the surface. He'd come up barking.

He thoroughly enjoyed walking the shore with us, whether it was the small, rocky beach along Pleasant Street or out on Cornelius Island, where we used to go clamming for long-necks or soft-shelled clams as we called them.

Bill would patrol the shallow waters, seeking out the crabs. When he spotted one, he'd stick his head underwater and snatch the thing by the side of its shell. He'd head for shore with his prize. The crab would be pinching his face and Bill would whine and growl at the same time. He'd carry the crab far from shore and drop it. The crab would turn and start walking toward the water. Bill would dig furiously between the crab and the water. The crab would fall into his hole and land upside down.

Bill would leave, satisfied, and go look for more prey. He didn't seem to notice that the crabs used their long tails to right themselves and get back to the water.

I read in that same article that the tail of the horseshoe crab, while hard and menacing-looking, is not dangerous. They use it for steering in water and for righting themselves when they get tipped over.

That's not the way we used to hear it as kids. Parents would warn us not to dive head-first from the raft at Cold Spring Beach as we might be impaled by the tail of a horseshoe crab. That may not be true, but my advice when swimming in horseshoe crab territory is to stick with the cannonball. And try not to sink too deep.

#1 Rule for Ocean Safety: Stay in the Boat

Every once in a while, the Wickford Shellfish would be pressed into service to provide all the fixings for a good old New England lobster and clambake. This called for the lobsters and clams to be cooked in a pit lined with layers of rockweed.

That's where I came in. I got paid so much per burlap bag stuffed with rockweed. There were several reasons I enjoyed my rockweed job.

One was the extra money. Another was the pride of making money off the sea, so to speak. The best, though, was stacking my skiff sky high with bags of rockweed and putt-putting across the harbor with my "catch." To the uninitiated, it looked as if I had a world-record haul of clams. I even had someone shout across the water one time: "Are those quahogs!?!!" I couldn't lie, so I just gave him a non-committal shrug.

My favorite spot for collecting rockweed was along a rocky stretch of beach that lay west and northwest of Cornelius Island.

One morning, early, I anchored off shore because the tide was going out and I didn't want my boat to get beached. I waded to shore. As usual, there was no one else around. Every time I had two bags full, I would hoist them on my shoulders, wade back, deposit them in the boat and return to the beach for more.

Eventually the tide turned and the water got deeper. I was just about done, so I didn't move the boat, which by now was in chest-deep water. I had my last two bags on my shoulders and was walking through the water to the boat when I heard a shrill whistle. I didn't pay any heed and kept walking. Another sharp whistle. I kept walking and then heard a series of what sounded like very excited whistles. A short burst of them.

I stopped, waist deep in water, and looked in the general direction of where the whistles were coming from. I saw a clammer over by Cornelius island. He was waving and pointing at my boat.

I looked to where he was pointing and saw the unmistakable fin of a shark, a large shark, slicing between me and my boat.

Have you ever tried to run in deep water? I don't think it can be done, but I do believe I came as close as humanly possible that morning. It seemed to take me hours, but I know it was just seconds before I was safely on the beach, panting heavily, with my two burlap bags, somehow, still perched on my shoulders.

I watched as the shark circled and made another pass in front of my boat. I tried to calculate how big it was based on the portion of the shark that I could make out under the water. It seemed almost as long as my 14-foot boat. I watched it go out away from me until I calculated that I could make it safely to my boat.

There was another time when I was with my folks and we were heading back to land after a little fishing. The channel at one point passes right by the tip of Pleasant Street, which ends at the water.

I said I would swim to shore and jumped out. My folks continued on and I began paddling.

That's when I noticed the turmoil in the water, a couple of hundred yards away. From what I could tell from my poor vantage point, it appeared some men in two boats were chasing something in the water and trying to beat it at the same time.

You won't find it in any record books, but I covered the 50 yards to shore in a mind-boggling time. For whatever reason, the men in the boats were chasing a shark and pummeling it with long clamming rakes. They passed through the waters where I had been a short while earlier and continued on.

I walked the short distance home, determined that next time I would stick with the boat.

I Was a Teen-age Quahogger

His name was Paul and he lived in a house out next to a marshy tidal pool known as South Cove. If I had known the term back in the early 1960s, I would have considered him "squirrelly." We just called him an odd duck.

Paul was a quahogger and would sell his daily catch to the Wickford Shellfish. As I did with the other quahoggers, I would take Paul's burlap sacks, weigh them and pay him money, cash. No questions asked.

What I wouldn't do with Paul's quahogs is sell them to our retail customers. His were set aside for shipping up the road, to East Greenwich, where the wholesale companies were located that supplied the national canneries that made clam chowder.

Soon after I started work at the Shellfish, my boss, Eddie Archambault, showed me Paul's quahogs. The outside of the shells were whiter and chalkier than others. Eddie could tell from the shells where quahogs came from. These, he told me, came from South Cove, which was polluted.

Paul, he told me, dug his quahogs at night, which was illegal, and in polluted waters, also illegal.

Eddie bought them because, well, because Wickford was a small town. And Paul needed the money. To this day I avoid canned clam chowder.

Charlie Baker was another of our regular quahoggers. It hurt me to watch Charlie unload his catch. He was old and pretty much crippled up from a lifetime of quahogging.

The quahoggers tied up their boats to the long vertical poles that were sunk in the mud and held up the wooden pier that jutted out into the water. At high tide, the boats would be only a few feet below the pier. At low tide, they would be six feet or so lower than that.

When the tide was out, the quahogger would have to wrestle the burlap sacks holding his catch up a rickety ladder and place them one by one on the pier. Then he would fetch a dolly to wheel them inside to be weighed. We paid 11 cents a pound for small cherrystones and 5 cents a pound for the bigger, tougher chowder ones.

One day, soon after I started working at the shellfish, I knelt down on the pier at low tide and extended my hand down so Charlie could hand me his bags and I could place them on the pier. I didn't know how he'd react. These guys were, and still are, individualists.

But Charlie really appreciated the help. Before long, he would just tie up his boat and go join the other diggers in their daily bull session outside the back door of the shellfish. An assortment of old fish barrels and crates served as furniture. I would climb down into Charlie's boat and heave his catch up to the pier, haul it inside, weigh it and bring the money to Charlie, who would be relaxing in the shade.

The other quahoggers took note of this and I soon found myself helping them as well. It meant a lot to me that they never watched me weigh their catch and never counted their money in front of me. Their money came from a cash drawer and I took as much as I needed. Eddie never questioned my honesty.

The quahoggers would just hang around for a while most afternoons swapping stories. I didn't feel right taking the time to listen as I had work to do. This, on occasion, would infuriate Eddie, who would actually order me to sit down and take a break and listen.

He'd yell something like: "I'm your boss, damn it! Get over here and sit down!"

During one of these sessions someone asked Eddie about his younger days. He said that in the 1930s he was captain of a slave ship off the coast of Africa. Everyone else seemed to know what he was talking about and the subject was dropped. I didn't know and never asked. I wish I had.

I could tell the quahoggers respected Eddie, as did the lobstermen.

The local lobster boats set their traps in Narragansett Bay. This gave us a steady supply of the smaller lobsters and sometimes other things.

One of the boats came in one day with an enormous swordfish. I managed to drag the heavy fish out of the boat, onto a dolly and into the shop. As a reward, Eddie sliced a very thick slice off, wrapped it in paper and gave it to me. Mom spread butter on it and broiled it in the oven for the night's supper.

Eddie also bought lobsters from a much bigger ocean-going lobster boat that trawled the waters in the Georges Banks area.

I was pressed into service early one Sunday morning after this boat had docked at Point Judith on the southern tip of Rhode Island. The boat and crew had been to sea for much longer than a few days. We unloaded a lot of lobsters that morning. When we were done, I was standing with Eddie as he counted out and handed the captain $14,000 in $100 bills. To somebody whose head was still spinning because he was making $1.50 an hour, this seemed incredible.

Eddie had told me that this captain was purported to be the best at guessing where to find the deep-sea lobsters, which can be hard to locate. The captain related to Eddie he had such a good catch because he was able to elude several other lobster boats that were intent on following him. He had departed at night and then sought out whatever fog banks he could find along the way to give them the slip. It worked.

The Wickford Shellfish changed hands after my second summer and I was once again in search of work.

Charlie Baker came to my rescue. He had a spare quahogging boat that was beached and in need of serious work. I could borrow it, Charlie told me, if I could get it all patched, which I did.

I was a quahogger. I was thrilled. I was proud.

I had learned a lot listening to the quahoggers. But I had a lot more to learn.

After you reach a chosen spot to work, you toss out your anchor and let out rope. Your boat will drift back and forth with winds and tide at the end of the rope. After that area is fished, you pull the rope in a few feet (shorter) and repeat. After doing this a few times, you pull up anchor, get to a new spot and do it all over again.

A few of the guys used bull rakes, which they tossed out and dragged through the mud. This took a lot of strength. I chose to use tongs, big metal baskets tipped with sharp teeth. You work these back and forth gathering clams in a pile that you can't see but that can feel down there in the sand and muck. When you feel that you have a sufficient pile, you scoop them up by gently tossing them with an up motion, opening and closing tongs, and then snatching them and pulling them up. It's all done by feel.

When the tongs are pulled up, you need to rest the top handle on a pole so the tongs will stay open and you can pluck out the quahogs.

I was doing this and getting wet. Hazard of the job, I figured. Charlie Baker stopped by my boat one day and told me if I fished off the other side of the boat I wouldn't get wet.

The wind was blowing the water off my tongs onto me. By going to the other side of the boat, I would be upwind of the tongs and the water would blow away from me.

I also noticed one day that the quahoggers were heading in early and all at once as well. Charlie was among them, but took the time to detour to my boat.

"Thunderheads in southeast, rain in a half-hour," Charlie said tersely. "If you start in right now, you might make it before all hell breaks loose."

I didn't. Just a few hundred feet away from the sanctuary of the breakwater, the furious squall enveloped my small craft. Because of the swirling winds, the waves attacked from every direction.

At times I would be surrounded by angry waves, unable to see anything but water in all directions. Then I would ride a wave up to a crest so narrow that the propeller on my outboard motor would come out of the water. Then I would plunge back down.

I had to steer directly into whichever wave was the closest. If I hit it head on, I was OK. If it hit me sideways, I risked being swamped. This meant I had to zig-zag and not head directly for the breakwater.

Adding to my dilemma was the fact that my boat sprang a leak from the pounding. With one hand, I pushed some extra caulking between the planks. This slowed the water down but didn't stop it as I continued to have a plume squirting into the air. The rain was pounding as well. Steering with one hand, I bailed with the other.

I zigged and zagged and made the calmer waters inside the breakwater. After that experience, I kept an eye on the southeast.

How Not to Throw a Boarding Party

I ignored the U.S. Coast Guard boat I could feel over my shoulder and whoever it was barking "Heave to!" through a megaphone.

Certainly, I thought, they have better things to do than harass a poor shellfisher heading to port with his day's catch of quahogs. Pretend you don't hear them. Just keep going, I said to myself.

One of the Coast Guardsmen made a nice throw with his rope and got my boat lassoed by the prow.

An officer, I assumed, ordered me to kill my engine and then loudly commanded: "Prepare for a boarding party!"

When you're transporting contraband, as I happened to be, these are not the words you want to hear.

I started the day quahogging due east from Cold Spring beach. I was working my tongs in waters that were about 10-feet deep. As usual, I was sorting my shellfish by sizes into two burlap sacks. If the quahog fit through the smaller of two rings, it was too small – or illegal – and had to be tossed back. But if it was, first, legal and then also fit through the larger of two rings, it qualified as a cherrystone and paid 11 cents a pound. If it was bigger than that, it was a chowder clam and paid 5 cents a pound.

In practice, a quahogger can eyeball the differences in almost all cases, resorting to the measuring rings only for close calls.

I always tossed the illegal ones back, until that day. For whatever reason, the spot I was quahogging was loaded with clams that were barely illegal. There were so many, that after a while I quit tossing them back and began setting them aside in a metal bucket. I reasoned that at the end of the day, if I had enough for supper for my parents and me I'd take them home. If not, I would toss them back.

I ended up with a nice haul. I felt Mom and Dad would appreciate a tasty clam supper. I knew they wouldn't notice that they were a tad on the illegal side.

Heading in, I placed a cushion on my pail and sat on it to conceal the evidence, just in case.

That was the position I was in when the Coast Guard officer, in a nicely pressed uniform, boarded my poor boat. For obvious reasons, I stayed seated and he didn't seem to mind my rudeness.

I showed him my papers, which were in order, and thought things were going well. Then he asked me to demonstrate my fog horn. Fog horn? He wasn't smiling.

He asked me to turn on my running lights. Lights? His frown deepened.

Then he wanted to see my life preserver. Not good. He shook his head and began writing me up for my offenses. Please, I thought, don't ask me what's in the bucket I'm sitting on. I was holding my breath when out of nowhere a demon in a speedboat appeared, heading straight for the Coast Guard boat.

At the last second, the speedboat veered off, sending a wall of water up onto the boat's deck, and sped away. The driver may have presented the crew with an obscene gesture as well.

The officer couldn't get me my ticket fast enough, ripping it from his book and tossing it in my direction before leaping back aboard his boat. A crewman quickly untied our line and off they sped, in hot pursuit of this new quarry.

I could have told them they were wasting their time. It was a neighbor, Bruce, and his family's boat was *FAST*.

After I made it home safely with supper, I was outside when I saw my benefactor. I thanked him profusely for coming to my rescue.

"It looked like you needed help," he said. He made a clean getaway. "They never had a chance."

The bad news came in the mail. A letter from the Coast Guard in Boston said the fines for my three offenses totaled $200. That represented a huge chunk of my income from a summer of quahogging.

But there appeared to be a ray of hope. The letter said the Coast Guard commandant could waive the fine if I presented satisfactory proof that I had righted my evil ways.

I showed my ticket to Ralph Northrup at the shipyard right behind our house. Ralph said things like ee-yeah-ah for yes. The real deal.

He fetched a small, inexpensive flashlight from his inventory and wrote "running lights" on my receipt. Then he produced a small, plastic toy that could be tooted by mouth. He wrote "fog horn."

There was no cheap way around the other thing, Ralph said solemnly. He brought out an expensive life preserver and added it to my list.

"Now," he explained. "If you decide, after sending your receipt to the Coast Guard, that you don't want this particular life preserver, you can bring it back, unopened, and I'll refund your money. Can't do that, though, with the flashlight and horn."

And that's how I ended up with a letter from the Commandant waiving my fine, a new flashlight, a neat, little toy horn, no life preserver and a delicious clam supper.

Insignificant Events

It was supper time and Dad was munching away at the kitchen table in our tiny project house. It must have been something special, but I don't remember what. What I do remember, vividly, is Mom asking: "Do you like it?"

To which Dad replied, unwisely: "I'm eatin' it, ain't I?"

To which Mom responded by hurling a salt shaker from across the table. It thumped off his chest. I wonder if she was aiming higher. Such things just didn't happen in our house and it made an impression on me and my brothers. Supper was finished quickly and silently. I carried this lesson throughout life: Never insult the cook, especially one you're married to.

I find it interesting that recollections of people in our lives are comprised of a series of such seemingly insignificant events. (I know my daughter Sarah will be forever telling people she learned to swear by listening, in bed, to "Santa" trying to assemble toys on Christmas Eve.) This is how it is with my father, who was Irish and had the legendary temper that goes with the bloodline. That is what I enjoyed the best.

Sometime in the early '50s we got a television. It was forever going on the blink and Dad would call John Kulawkowski to come over to fix it. This got to be a running gag – behind his back – as the TV would magically fix itself by the time Mr. Kulakowski got there. Soon after he would leave, it would go on the blink again. This would drive Dad into fits of off-color sputtering, and that was better entertainment than anything on TV.

Dad was proud of his radio. It was a table model, probably dating to the 1930s. The kind with a rounded top, solid wood, that you see now in antique stores. He was forever tinkering with it as it seemed always in need of special attention. Just as soon as he'd get it working and fine tuned, another tube or capacitor or resistor or something would go out.

One night, he got his beloved radio all set up on the kitchen table of our Pleasant Street house. There must have been something good he wanted to hear. He turned the radio on, apparently expecting it to perform flawlessly. Nothing happened.

Dad thumped it, then thumped it again, harder. Nothing. The radio had pushed him to the breaking point.

He picked it up and hurled it onto the floor. His precious radio split open. To the tune of "you god-damn son-of-a-bitch," Dad kicked it across the kitchen to the cellar door and then kicked it down the stairs. He followed it down the stairs, still swearing at it, and kicked it some more. It was finished. It lay in a pile of shattered wood and broken glass and twisted wires. The radio would taunt him no more.

Dad also was forever working on the 3.6 horsepower Evinrude motor that we used to power our 14-foot wooden skiff. They're are pretty basic motors, but Dad liked fooling with it anyway.

This boat motor, just like the TV and radio, seemed to have his number. It always ran great when we kids were using it. But when Dad went out for a solo trip, the little engine that could suddenly couldn't. Or, in Dad's world, wouldn't.

I don't think he ever appreciated how far voices carry across water. He'd be out in the boat, fairly far from shore, and we would be in the house and hear his unmistakeable "god-damn son-of-bitch" echoing through the neighborhood.

Everyone could hear it. We'd go outside and walk across the street to see him standing in the rear of the boat and pulling on the starting cord. Pulling and pulling. Answered by a sputter and a sputter. Answered by more cussing. We never told Dad how much we, and the neighbors, enjoyed his shows. It probably wouldn't have been wise to do so after he had rowed all the way in.

Another time, my brother Bob was supposed to be out of the Army and home, but wasn't. His tour had been extended because of the Berlin Crisis of 1961 and he had been shipped over to Germany. That's where he was at Christmas.

This brought Dad to the Post Office to mail a Christmas package. I was with him. The man at the Post Office window told Dad he couldn't mail the package until he filled out some official form stating what was in the box. Certain things were prohibited, you know.

Dad asked something like, "How come?" The clerk said it was a German thing. Dad flew into an all-out rage, creating quite the scene. His Army son was living in a tent on the front line in Germany protecting Berlin from the Russians. And the Germans were telling him what he could put in a

Christmas package?

He yelled for all to hear that he could send his son any god-damn thing he wanted. Referring to WWII, he screamed: "Who do you think won that god-damn war anyway? C'mon! Let's get out of here!"

We drove up the road to another town and another Post Office, which accepted the package with no questions asked and no form needed. I don't know, but I think the first Post Office may have called ahead.

I failed to mention that Dad always came home from work at 5 p.m., never used a sick day in 30-plus years at Quonset Point Naval Air Station, went to church every Sunday and kept the old church bus running, gratis, with his mechanical skills, contributed faithfully to the Red Cross blood drives, was a Boy Scout leader, helped coach my Babe Ruth baseball team and was awfully proud of his three sons. But who wants to write about that kind of stuff?

Sea Monsters

It was a good two hours before dawn that summer day in 1962 when I untied the family's 14-foot skiff from its moor just a short walk from our Pleasant Street house and slipped quietly from the sheltered cove out into the harbor.

Not wanting to disturb anyone's slumber, I rowed until a comfortable distance from shore whereupon I tugged the cord of our tiny outboard motor, which sprang to life. I putt-putted out beyond the breakwater into Narragansett Bay. I had no lights. A sliver of moonlight showed me the way.

I had no reason to be there, except that I loved being out on the water in the cool and the dark, poking around with nowhere to go, inhaling the smells, taking it all in. I did this quite often, getting in some fishing for striped bass after sunup and getting back, refreshed, in time to begin my workday at 8 a.m.

I remember this particular day because I was scared out of my wits, by a celebrity of sorts.

I had turned off my little motor and was just drifting along with the tide, contemplating and pondering. I took note of some long pieces of sea grass floating with me. Just beyond that was something in the dim light that appeared to be big, very big. Much bigger than my boat, in fact. A log, perhaps?

That's odd, I thought. I never once recalled seeing big

pieces of driftwood in the bay. Then I noticed the "log" was wide and had a few ripples coming out from its side, as if it was doing more than just drifting. Why yes, I remember thinking, it is moving. And faster than me and the grass. And, oh my, I observed next, it's not drifting at all. It's moving *against* the tide.

Omigod! That's not a log! It's alive! And, by now, just a foot or two away!

I jumped to the back of the boat to start the motor before this monster, whatever it was, got me. I never before put any thought into how to start the motor. I always went through the motions automatically. But now, it seemed, I didn't know what to do. Panic had set in.

How do I start this damn thing? Think, damn it!

Somehow, it started. I gunned it and turned so sharply that I nearly fell overboard. Safely away, heart pounding, I pondered what kind of sea monster I had encountered. I wasn't going back to check it out.

Later, I heard the news. A whale, a rarity for Rhode Island waters, was seen exploring Narragansett Bay and making its way, slowly, toward Providence. Someone in the news business dubbed it Willy the Whale. Everyone was kept informed of the whale's progress for several days. It headed farther and farther away from the open ocean, finally reaching the iffy waters of the Providence River.

Not good for a whale and, alas, the story did not have a happy ending. But it always felt like my whale, cuz I seen it first. That counts for something.

It was three years later that I was working at Hal Thompson's Richfield Station on the Seattle waterfront when I had another whale thing happen.

Ted Griffen owned and operated a public aquarium across the street from our garage. He was a regular, bringing his truck in for gasoline and service.

Ted was in the news because he brought a killer whale to his aquarium and named it Namu. This was a first. He then brought in a female whale that he named Shamu. The two didn't get along, so he shipped Shamu to some upstart aquarium in San Diego that had just opened and was called something like SeaWorld. Shamu was its first Orca.

Ted gave me some tickets one day, so I went to his Sunday show. Namu was confined in a crude pen beside a wharf on Puget Sound. Spectators watched from the docks.

Griffen, in an act I felt to be foolhardy, jumped in with a snorkel, and wearing a wetsuit, put Namu through his paces. The grand finale was riding the whale's back, underwater. I was impressed by his courage and greatly relieved when he eventually surfaced.

The whole thing was controversial. There were "Free the Whale" protests by people who were concerned over Namu's captivity. Shortly after I caught the show, Namu became entangled in the cage and drowned. Another very sad ending to a whale story.

A Beginner's Guide to College

A friend suggested to me in the mid-1960s that I should quit wasting time as a journalism student at Seattle University and go to work for the Boeing aircraft company.

The aircraft business seemed to have two cycles – boom or bust – and this was one of the boom times. They were hiring laborers, my friend told me, and there was so much work that all the overtime you wanted was there for the taking. Double-time and even triple-time.

A common laborer? *Moi*?

I had worked as a dishwasher and soda jerk at a Howard Johnson's and pumped gas a LaBelle's Garage in Narragansett, RI, and had done the heavy lifting at the Wickford Shellfish Company and pumped more gas and parked cars at Hal Thompson's Richfield on the Seattle waterfront. No more, I told my friend.

I insisted on wasting four-plus years in college, not leaving until I had a degree and, incidentally, no money left after paying my last quarter's tuition.

While writing this here rant, I stumbled on the College Drop-out Hall of Fame website.

It says on the website: "I'm a firm believer that most college students would be better off dropping out of school and investing the money they now spend on college. Then take the four years they would have spent on college and travel, work, play, and spend time with smart people talking about important things.

"It would be your choice on what's important, not a pro-fessor, not a dean, not a faculty committee."

Amen, I say.

Will someone please tell me why I had to spend four years in college to become a newspaper reporter? Did I really have to do that to achieve the newspaper gold stand-ard – writing at the sixth grade level?

Don't think so. I think a one-week apprentice program would make most people over-qualified.

I blame my oldest brother, Bob, for my errant direction in this matter.

He informed our parents in 1955 that he was going to Providence College after graduating from La Salle Academy.

Dad went ballistic. He didn't want any son of his wasting time in college when they should be out working. He said so, emphatically, and laced with the most powerful cuss words at his disposal.

I'm not sure that Dad, who left the education environ-ment at 16, saw the need for even a high school diploma. He seemed suspicious of books and was less than happy when I came home one day with a library card.

Bob won the college argument, though, and things even-tually calmed down. The fact that he was going to enroll (for a brief time, it turned out) in pre-med may have had something to do with the peace treaty.

So it seemed natural, even noble, for me to follow in his footsteps. To college, that is.

I stuck it out at Seattle University and this is how I came

with a degree in journalism to my first newspaper job as News Editor at the Omak Chronicle.

I should point out that while newspapers are niggardly with pay they are very generous with titles. I was News Editor not because I was in charge of anyone. I was it. My business card actually could have read Peter Pegnam, News Staff.

Down the road at other newspapers I carried such lofty titles as Executive Editor, Editor, Copy Editor, State Editor and Wire Editor.

One thing the positions shared was the pay, or lack of pay, I should say.

Back to Omak. I showed up by Greyhound bus, deposited, after an all-night journey, at the side of the road with my belongings stuffed into a pillowcase. My boss picked me up, shook his head, gave me an advance, and let me borrow his old pickup truck until I could find my own transportation.

I found a room to rent over the pool hall, eager to cash in on my higher education.

It never happened. Twenty-eight years and four newspapers later I was making the same pay, adjusted for inflation.

Adding insult to injury, to this day I get mailings from Seattle University looking for money or an endowment or something. I tried telling them I was deceased, but that didn't stop the mailings. They are relentless.

Shouldn't they be sending me money?

Over the course of my distinguished journalism career, I thought a lot about doing something else. This led me to ponder quitting the news business and buying a food cart so I could sell hot dogs at county fairs and such.

I considered buying a tree pruning business until the broker handling the sale agreed with me that this line of work wasn't meant for someone afraid of heights.

I once sent away for information on becoming a long-distance truck driver. I liked that idea so much and talked about it so enthusiastically that one of my co-workers and golfing buddies, Clyde Foster, actually took my brochure from North American Van Lines, quit his job and left to drive a truck.

North American taught him how to drive an 18-wheeler in a matter of weeks. Not four years. He didn't have to study and pass a course on the history of the Roman Empire.

When he tired of being on the road, he settled down in North Dakota, where he bought a business specializing in small appliance repair. The previous owner didn't ask to see his college degree before selling him the business.

An acquaintance of mine once told me how he happened to drive through the faculty parking lot soon after he enrolled in college and saw a less than impressive array of cars. He remembered thinking: These are the people who are going to show me the way to fame and fortune? He quit after one semester.

A fast learner, he.

I am a slow learner, but finally did escape the newspaper business after nearly 30 years, eventually owning and running three businesses simultaneously with my wife. Someone stopped me one day in the parking lot of our modest cabin resort and asked if I was "the proprietor." I took an instant liking to that word. It has, to me, an air to it.

As a proprietor I had to perform a certain amount of manual labor, such as firewood splitting and stacking, snow shoveling, barbecue grill cleaning, furniture moving, plumbing and minor repairs. I was at long last satisfied. My friend from college had been right all along. A higher education had not been necessary.

First Impressions

I know I looked a little rough when I showed up for my job interview at the Omak Chronicle that December day in 1966.

But Bruce Wilson – editor, publisher, owner, boss – was, well, downright shabby.

At least I had an excuse. I had boarded a late-afternoon bus in Seattle for the long ride across the Cascade Mountains. When we arrived, well after dark, at the bus station in Wenatchee, I was the only passenger to get off. The small bus station was deserted and I made myself as comfortable as I could for the night on the hard wooden benches.

When first light finally dawned I wandered down the street, eventually finding a diner that was just opening for the day.

The Greyhound bus bound for Omak, some 90 miles to the north along the Okanogan River, picked me up with a handful of other pilgrims. I stared at the bleak winter landscape passing by and second-guessed my decision to even agree to a job interview.

Tired and bleary-eyed, I walked a short distance to the Chronicle building on Main Street to meet Bruce, who, it appeared, had not shaved for several days and was attired in a tattered flannel shirt, badly worn pants and beat-up shoes.

We squeezed in a visit and lunch before the bus returned to pick me up for the trek back to the Coast.

A few days later a letter from Bruce arrived offering me the position of News Editor with the Chronicle. My doubts about Omak had evaporated during our brief meeting.

I was thankful that the Nome (Alaska) Nugget had already filled its position before my letter of inquiry arrived. And although you could still get a good mug of coffee for a nickel at the bowling alley in Nampa, Idaho, I was grateful The Idaho Free Press didn't want to take a chance on my uncertain draft status. And glad that The Daily Idahonian in Moscow had just filled its vacancy.

Bruce also sent me a copy of the week's paper, which had a story, by him, of the new Miranda warning that cops would be required to read to suspects. It included a posed picture of the sheriff reading the rights to a desperado.

Although you could see only the backside, I recognized the "bad guy" from his clothing. It was Bruce. That was why he had dressed that way. He was his own photo prop.

Another bus ride later, I arrived in Omak for my first newspaper job. It was Friday, the 13th, January 1967.

The departing Grant Heppenstall, who had spent but a few months in Omak after arriving from Ketchikan, Alaska, had just a couple of hours to show me around the town. Bruce gave me a notebook, a pencil and asked if I knew how to use a camera.

I didn't. He patiently explained in a period of about three minutes everything I needed to know about photography – the f stops and flash bulbs and how to put film in the camera and how to take it out and all that kind of technical stuff. He also mentioned that a weekly newspaper editor is on duty 24/7.

And, of course, he noted that whenever the town's siren went off summoning the volunteer firefighters to duty, I was expected to be where the action was with camera, note-book and pencil.

It was early the next morning, a Saturday, when I was awakened by the unmistakable wail of a siren.

I got dressed but didn't know what to do after that. Then I got lucky. I heard the fire trucks on the street right behind my room.

I walked out the door and around the corner and saw fire trucks and smoke. Putting my new-found skills to test, I snapped a picture. I struck up a conversation with a gentle-men, the local electrician it turned out, who was standing outside the smoking house. It was his house. He gave me all the details.

For Sunday, Bruce had kindly scheduled me to cover a snowmobile race out in the mountains. In the deep snow.

It didn't take me long to drive the boss's pickup truck with balding tires off the snowy, narrow, twisting back-woods road. Two young men winched out the truck and gave me a ride the rest of the way in their properly outfitted 4-wheel drive vehicle.

I took pictures of the races before a deputy sheriff took pity on my lack of proper winter clothing and let me sit with him in his patrol car to thaw out.

When I showed up at the newspaper office Monday morning, Bruce was impressed I had a picture and all the details on the Saturday fire. His pickup truck was undam-aged by its off-road venture, so I decided not to let him in on that one. Nor on how I had stumbled onto the fire and interview.

A snowmobile race picture was usable, even though the horizon was out of kilter.

I was getting off on the right foot.

Guide to Humor

When Bill Rowe saw the ad in 1961, he knew he had to apply for the job: "Wanted: Pressman to hunt, fish and loaf in the beautiful North Cascade Mountains, interrupted only by pleasurable eight-hour shifts at the Omak Chronicle."

He figured he'd probably like working for the person behind such a humorous ad. He figured right. And that was how Bill got to be shop foreman and pressman for Bruce Wilson, owner and publisher of the Chronicle and a humorist by any definition.

Bruce also left his mark on the Washington State Legislature.

When he announced his retirement from the Legislature after three terms in 1982, the headline in The Spokesman-Review newspaper in Spokane read: "Conscience of the Senate" retiring.

The article noted that the Washington state Senate was "losing a hunk of its conscience, its humility, its intellectual sharpness and its sense of humor.

"He's a man of few words – he rarely makes a floor speech but, unlike long-winded legislators who are ignored by their colleagues, people listen when Wilson talks."

Wilson, it added, "is legendary for his knack of cutting though the Senate's high-blown rhetoric to reveal fundamental truths by poking fun. Wilson isn't the only humorist in the Legislature, but he's one of the best."

Someone mailed me a copy of the article and I dropped Bruce a brief letter in which I noted all these wonderful qualities, adding in jest, "whatever happened to the Bruce Wilson I knew?"

Bruce replied warmly, noting that "surely you learned when you lived up here that you can't believe everything printed in the Spokesman."

Actually, the Spokesman was 100 percent right. He was all that stuff, and more.

He was smart, a solid journalist, excellent writer and a man of his word. Every once in a while, if we're lucky, we cross paths with someone who makes us a better person. The last time I saw him was 1970, and to this day I try to be more like Bruce, as a writer and as a man.

When Bruce hired me fresh out of college in 1967, he said his part of the bargain was that he would be around to train me and to spend about 20 hours a week working on the news side of the business.

I was sitting at my desk one day when Bruce stopped by and squatted down so we'd be on eye level. He told me he was considering running for the state Senate. He reminded me of his standing commitment to be there with me and for me and said that if I objected he wouldn't run. Period.

I knew he meant it. One hundred percent.

When he was absent during the legislative sessions, I would get letters of encouragement such as this from April 28, 1969: "I have carefully studied the Chronicle for April 24 and wish to comment on the large number of very good stories...The articles were extremely well handled and I am wondering who you got to write them." Pure Bruce.

And a 1970 note that concluded: "I am courteously interested in the welfare of your wife, daughter, and Child No. 2 but am really anxious to know how your dog is getting along."

After I left the Chronicle, I carried a sealed envelope with a letter from Bruce highly recommending me for a new position. The letter concluded with Bruce noting that my wife was actually better qualified, but she was busy with two kids and a dog to care for. I still managed to get the job.

Bruce managed to sneak his humor into the Chronicle in a variety of ways.

A one-sentence brief Bruce typed up read in its entirety: "Mr. and Mrs. Paul Maley have returned from a trip to Spokane, where they enjoyed a very expensive dinner."

This one nearly backfired on Bruce. Paul Maley was the owner of the town's appliance store. When the tiny story appeared, Maley's phone rang off the hook with the locals wanting to know what the scoop was behind the "expensive dinner."

Maley frequently bought large ads in the Chronicle for his business. He told Bruce that none of his big, expensive ads ever generated the response he got from this tiny story. He threatened, only half-jokingly, to reduce his advertising to one-inch spots.

Among Bruce's good friends were the Nelsons. He knew they would get a chuckle out of another little story he planted in the Chronicle: "Mr. and Mrs. Lester Nelson have returned from their European vacation. They will be showing slides of their trip at their home at 7 p.m. Friday." and then the kicker: "Refreshments will be served."

That was the first the Nelsons knew of any slide presenta-tion. *That* Bruce, they said. They laughed. But then they started to wonder if someone might take it seriously. Nobody would ever come to look at vacation slides, they reasoned. But, then again, what if people did show up?

They went out and bought refreshments, just in case. Bor-rowed some extra folding chairs, because you never know. Got the slides all organized to be on the safe side. As expec-ted, no one showed up.

They always laughed when re-telling the story.

At year's end, Bruce would put together for the Chronicle a humorous news quiz and a crossword puzzle with a local twist. One year he got boxed in with an impossible combin-ation of letters in one corner of the crossword puzzle. He solved his dilemma with an ingenious clue: "There has nev-er been a word like this, and never will be."

Bruce similarly saved the day for me one particular time that comes to memory. Early on, I took a picture of a check presentation and posed the two gentleman side-by-side, shaking hands and exchanging the check. I know you've seen similar pictures many times. It's a cliché. But I didn't know that. When I brought the picture back from the cam-era shop and he saw it, Bruce roared with laughter.

He saved the day with a cutline that started out with something like "OK. You think of another way to take this picture..."

Just after Bruce was elected to the Senate, one of the vet-eran legislators was teaching him the ropes. To get his feet wet, he had Bruce write up a small, inconsequential, non-controversial bill.

He showed Bruce how to make the rounds, ensuring all the right senators had copies of the bill and that the way was cleared for easy passage.

This was to be a simple, unanimous voice vote. On Bruce's big day one of the senators surprisingly asked for a roll call vote. Bruce wondered what that was all about. The roll call started.

Bruce became panic-stricken as he watched the roll call tallies add up. For some reason, many of the senators were voting "Nay." It was nip and tuck, down to the final vote, which went against the measure. Bruce's introductory legislation, a no-brainer, had failed. What had he done wrong?

Bruce loved to tell how he had been set up and had fallen for it. The whole Senate laughed and then reconsidered the bill, passing it unanimously.

Bruce enjoyed humor, even when it was at his expense.

When I was getting ready to cover the Okanogan County Fair for the first time, Bruce wanted to make sure I knew what the livestock auction was all about.

He told me that he didn't when the local Lions Club dispatched him and Ralph Mundinger to the fair to purchase the Grand Champion steer or something of the sort.

Bruce told me that he and Ralph couldn't believe how cheaply the animals were going for. Pocket change. The two buddies didn't realize that was the *per pound* price.

They were yucking it up pretty good when they started bidding. Ralph would bid $1 and Bruce would say $2 and up and up.

He noticed that others were giving them strange looks.

After the bidding, the men found out the Lions Club was

in hock for thousands of dollars.

Bruce, laughing, told me how relieved everyone was when the affair was amicably settled for much less than the actual bid.

Producing Three Crops Per Year

Did you ever wonder how much cotton it takes to make a t-shirt?

In Arizona, which produces a lot of cotton, farmers get close to 1,500 pounds of cotton per acre – or enough to make some 3,600 t-shirts.

And when you consider that, at latest count, 200,000 acres of Arizona land were planted in cotton, that's a lot of t-shirts.

I became interested in this topic after moving to Pinal County, which is Arizona's largest cotton-producing area.

I also found out what a cotton gin really is. Oh, well. I further discovered that the farmers plant in March or April and begin their harvest in early November.

One cotton crop per year. So far, so good.

My first brush with agriculture, other than a backyard garden, came in apple country in Okanogan County in Washington State.

I had just landed my first newspaper job, with the Omak Chronicle. I had to write about a lot of things I knew nothing about. Apple growing was one of these.

During the course of a couple of years, I began to see a pattern to my apple stories.

It had to do with the number of crops that the orchardists produced in a year. I have on occasion since then mentioned to people that some of the apple growers in Washington could produce three crops a year.

Folks find this hard to believe, until I explain.

It seems in the spring there would be a late frost that would nip the precious little apple blossoms in the bud, as it were.

A few phone calls from the Omak Chronicle would confirm the extent of the damage: "Wiped out. Disaster. Won't get a single apple this year." I would write a story. No apples this year.

Amazingly, to me but to no one else, apples soon would begin to appear on the trees.

But wouldn't you know it? Late summer would bring a ferocious, pounding hailstorm.

More phone calls: Goodness! "Nary an apple left. Remaining ones all damaged. May be able to sell a few as culls." Another story. Crop Number 2 wiped out. Gone.

Somehow, though, the harvest would eventually begin. On schedule, transient apple-pickers would appear throughout the county and take up residence under bridges along the Okanogan River.

They would pick what a non-skeptic might call the magical third crop of the year.

And by all accounts it would be a good one because the next batch of stories on the apple growers would be about their winter holidays in Scottsdale, Arizona.

O Christmas Tree

I think it was my first December in Omak that the plan emerged to go up into the Okanogan National Forest and cut down a live Christmas tree. How idyllic it seemed.

With the assistance of studded snow tires, my '59 Chevy made it to the nearest tree-cutting area somewhere up above Conconully. The forest was buried in a mere two or three feet of snow. Oh, what fun.

In no time at all, I found the perfect specimen. Isn't it amazing how small a tree looks out in its natural environment when it is surrounded by towering Ponderosa pines? The official regulations on my permit placed a maximum height on a tree. I thought this one would be OK. It wasn't.

The rules also said I had to leave a stump of only so many inches. This required digging down through the snow to the ground. I didn't seem to notice that this added two or three feet to the height.

With no little amount of sawing and chopping and sweating, I managed to fell my tree. Timber-r-r-r.

The next step was to drag it through the snow to the car. That was when I got my first hint that this beauty may have been bigger than allowed. It was heavy. Walking through deep snow is hard enough, but doing it and dragging a tree at the same time was not this idyllic adventure I imagined. It now seemed border-line idiotic. OK. Scratch border-line.

My next clue as to the size of this thing was that it

wouldn't fit in the very large trunk of my car, even leaving the lid up.

It had to go on the roof. After I wrestled it up there and got it secured is when I noticed that it hung out way past the windshield. The '59 Chevy was a big car, and this was definitely a big tree. Maybe a 14-footer for a house with an eight-foot ceiling.

Fortunately, I encountered no tree police on the journey home. That's where the problems really started.

I managed to drag it through the door. When I tried to stand it up, it was obvious that the tree needed some trimming. It was too tall. A lot too tall.

I apparently was off somewhere goofing around when God was handing out these genes to all the other guys that let them see the easy, simple, common sense way to do things around the house.

This is why I said to myself: "The tree is hitting the ceiling. That's where the problem is. Let's lop off a couple of feet from the top of the tree and then it won't be hitting the ceiling."

Simple. As any idiot can see.

Two feet off the top wasn't nearly enough. So I cut some more and then some more. I eventually got it so it would stand up, but there was no space on top for the star. So I trimmed a little more. Finally, I was done and took a few steps back to admire my work.

To my horror, I discovered that by taking off the pointy end up on top I had created a perfectly square Christmas tree.

We decorated it anyway. Now, wouldn't you think that a

tree that had the same shape as a National Football League lineman would be sturdy? For some reason, my square tree was very unsteady.

Soon after it was decorated, in fact, it fell flat onto the floor. Nothing seemed to work until I looped a rope around it and tied it to a heavy piece of furniture.

This experience naturally led me thereafter to visit tree lots and pay any price for the stalest, scrawniest tree. It didn't matter. It was worth the dough.

Three decades of living apparently blurred my memory sufficiently that when Janet suggested during our first Christmas season together that we cut a fresh tree, I said: "What a great idea!"

And for several years we did have some fun tree-cutting outings with kids and grand kids, going out into the Apache National Forest near Greer, AZ.

The last year we did this, Janet and I were alone. The snow was deep and we thought we might have to forgo the adventure. With a little patience, though, we found a place we could get our 4x4 SUV into.

I was relieved that the cold weather had created a firm crust on the snow and I could walk on top of it.

"Look, Janet, I can walk on snow!" I believe those were my last words before I plunged through.

It was waist deep. For the next hour, we would walk through the deep snow until we found a hard surface. Then we would walk on top of the snow until we fell through. I was not singing "Fa-la-la-la-la-la-la."

We got the tree. A few days after that Christmas, we were in a store that had an artificial tree on sale. We bought it.

Small-town Journalism 101

I have a well-worn, cherished card identifying me as a Cochise County Deputy Sheriff.

It was signed and given to me by Cochise County Sheriff Jim Willson during the time I was employed by the Sierra Vista (Ariz.) Herald-Dispatch. "If you ever need one of my deputies to give you a ride anywhere in the county, day or night," Willson told me, "just show them this card, and they'll take you."

My introduction to the sheriff came soon after I started work in 1970. I ran into him in the County Courthouse in Bisbee and he wanted to give me a tour of the area.

We got in his squad car and headed for the tiny border town of Naco. At the border entry post, we turned onto a dirt road and headed east. The wall separating the United States and Mexico quickly gave way to a barbed wire fence. A short distance later, the barbed wire fence turned into remnants.

We stopped and stepped over a single strand of wire. "We're now illegal aliens, in Mexico," the sheriff said. He laughed at the lack of security, which was widely unknown outside the border areas in those days.

There in the Mexican desert, Willson lifted one of his cowboy boots to show me the X he had carved in the heel. He was an excellent tracker, as were many of his deputies. They carved emblems into the heels of their boots so they would recognize each other's tracks.

The cowboy boots were part of the uniform. Willson told me that when people came to Cochise County – the land of Wyatt Earp, Doc Holliday and the OK Corral – they expected to see lawmen with a western look. And that's what he provided.

Uniforms were western hats, boots and jeans. He wasn't particularly overjoyed when a deputy handed out a traffic ticket. Some people might view drivers going over the posted limit as speeders. Jim viewed them as potential voters.

Jim hardly knew me but was not shy about sharing his philosophy of law enforcement. This involved what he called moonlight extraditions, a prisoner exchange of sorts with the Mexican police. They got somebody they wanted; and Willson got somebody he wanted.

The prisoners were directed at gunpoint to walk across the border; or not. Willson laughed when he told me that they all chose to cross the border and face the music, not his six-shooter.

He told me that once a year he would saddle up and ride the Cochise County part of the international border end to end. "The sheriff needs to know his territory."

It was later said that the Cochise County Sheriff's Department did not enter the 20th century until Jimmy Judd was elected sheriff in 1976. I think Willson would have considered it a compliment to be told he was operating the department as if it were the 1880s.

Someone in the county attorney's office told me one time that on occasion an old cowboy friend of Willson's would be down on his luck and come to Jim for help. The sheriff would see that he had a gun, swear him in on the spot and hand him a badge.

The attorney cringed at the potential liability.

I can't recall the details, but it was during this era that one deputy fatally shot another deputy during a quick draw contest at the Bowie substation. To settle an argument about who was faster, the deputies unloaded their guns and drew.

Tragically, one of the guns was not totally empty and accidentally fired.

Another deputy, considered to be an expert gunsmith, was prevailed upon to maintain weapons for the men on the force. During a visit to the Sierra Vista substation, he accidentally discharged a shotgun, which fired across the room and struck a metal chair. This hit home, as I sometimes sat in that chair when visiting the office.

There was other minor excitement in the Sierra Vista substation one day when an angry parent called to demand his son be released from custody and sent home. If the boy was not home by a certain time, the dad said, "I'm going to strap on my gun and come down there and find out the reason why."

They told him to come ahead. They also called me and invited me to come over with notebook and camera as they thought "something interesting" might happen. I went. Fortunately, the father had cooled off somewhat by the time he got there, kept his six-shooter holstered, and accepted the officers' explanation about the situation.

On days when I needed to get out of the newspaper office for a spell, I'd head over to the Sierra Vista substation and visit Frank, the deputy in charge and a good lawman whose company I always enjoyed.

He also was usually anxious to get out of the office and we'd go for a ride. Things seemed to happen when we got together.

One quiet afternoon when we were out in his squad car, a call came in of a burglary in process at a rural home. We went speeding down Highway 92, his older model patrol car vibrating to near the breaking point.

We pulled up in front, got out and started to walk toward the house when Frank spotted movement inside. He drew his large six-shooter and went running toward the front door.

He hollered at me to "cover the back!" I did as directed. As I was coming around the rear of the house, I heard Frank in the house yelling "Freeze!" Just then the back door slammed open and a young man burst through, making a run for it.

Instinctively, I guess, I went into a crouch, pointed my index finger in his direction and hollered FREEZE in the deepest, most menacing voice I could muster at that moment.

The desperado, not having time to study the caliber of my index finger, stopped on a dime. "Inside!" I ordered, getting the hang of things.

He meekly complied and returned to the living room, where Frank had his two friends at gunpoint. They were teenagers, unarmed. Frank handcuffed them and took them in with me riding shotgun, as it were.

It amazes me how much law enforcement has changed since then. Another day I was with Frank when a police raid was quickly organized.

Word had come in that a couple wanted in connection with a lawman's shooting in Florida were staying in a local motel room.

There was no concept of a SWAT team or a call to the room in an attempt to coax them out. This tactic involved four patrol cars roaring into the parking lot.

As we raced in, Frank calmly asked me: "Do you want a gun?" I declined. "There's one in the glove compartment if you want," he said. I appreciated his concern, but thought better of it.

I opted instead to bail out of the car after it screeched to a stop and crouch down behind it.

One of the deputies knocked on the motel room door. When it had barely cracked open, he reached one hand inside and grabbed a man by the shirt collar, jerked him through the doorway, spun him around and slammed him against the wall. All in one quick motion. I was impressed.

Inside were several weapons, including a loaded shotgun. His lady friend was concerned with this turn of events, but really upset about what would happen to their dog. She asked if she could find a neighbor to take care of it. One of the deputies, figuring I could be spared, ordered me to stay with her, which I did. I stayed by her side as she knocked on doors, eventually finding a woman to care for her dog. Thank goodness she didn't make a break for it.

I had another uneasy situation with a raid involving Sierra Vista police. They invited me along for an early morning drug raid on a home in Huachuca city. The cars stopped on the side of the road on the outskirts of town. No one said much as the officers got out, took an assortment of shotguns from the trunk of one car, checked to make sure everything was loaded and ready, got in and rode on, heavily armed and in silence, to their destination.

The cars pulled in, quickly, and I found myself in the rear seat looking out the window directly into window of the house just a few feet away. That was not a comfortable feeling. The door was kicked in and the sleepy inhabitants roused and rounded up.

Huachuca City was in the news again one day when the Arizona Attorney General decreed the small town to be a speed trap. To get from Sierra Vista or Fort Huachuca to I-10 and Tucson, motorists had to pass through Huachuca City, which relied on traffic fines for a good portion of the town budget.

There was always a Huachuca City cop lurking where the road went downhill, where the speed limit suddenly dropped, and where there were a couple of really good hiding places. Many ticket recipients swore they were cited even though they were going well under the limit.

I didn't manage to make contact with the police chief, with whom I had a very cordial relationship, before rushing the news release into the paper.

That was Friday afternoon. On Saturday, it dawned on me that I had to drive to Tucson. I crept through Huachuca City. And, of course, on the side of the road was a cop car. It pulled out after me with red lights and even a siren. They knew my car.

I stopped and looked in the mirror to see the chief himself getting out of his car, tugging on and adjusting his gunbelt as if he meant business.

He leaned down, squinted, paused for dramatic effect and said: "I thought that would scare you." He was right. We shared a laugh and I got his side of the story in the next edition.

It still seems amazing to me that in the 1967-70 years that I was in Omak, I was, as near as I could tell, the semi-official photographer for the Omak Police and Fire departments, the Okanogan County Sheriff's Department and the local office of the Washington State Patrol.

Whenever there was a traffic fatality, for example, any hour of the day or night, I would be there. At times, I would get a call in the middle of the night from the dispatcher telling me that a squad car was heading to a bad accident and would stop at my house to pick me up on the way. I would dress quickly and be waiting at the curb.

At the scene, I would take a picture that would tell the story of what happened in a manner suitable for a family newspaper. Then I would ask the officer what pictures he wanted me to take. These could be quite gruesome. The newspaper would provide copies of these photos gratis. They got their photos and the Chronicle got the story. A symbiotic relationship.

The Omak Fire Chief had my car outfitted with the same flashing blue lights behind the grill that the volunteers fire fighters had. That way I could make it to the fire to get pictures, for the paper and for the department.

At times, I got to the fire before the trucks. So the chief asked me for a favor in that regards. If it was a house fire and there was someone around, could I try to find out if there was someone inside? That way, I could alert the crews when they got there, saving precious time.

One last war story. The fire sirens blared just after dawn that day, usually a bad sign that a fire smoldering overnight had just been noticed. That was the case this time and it involved Omak's bowling alley.

A burning bowling alley is a spectacular sight. The wooden lanes, highly varnished, provide lots of fuel. When this smoldering fire inside got hot enough, it burst a window which let in a whoosh of fresh air – oxygen – and the flames exploded.

I found myself running backwards to get far enough away so I could get the whole towering smoke column in the frame of my camera.

I then found myself at the end of the bowling alley with the Okanogan fire crews who had come up from the neighboring town to assist. They threw a ladder against the wall and climbed onto the roof. With the permission of the chief, who I knew, I followed.

The roof started making unsettling noises and everyone rushed for the ladder down. As everyone was scrambling, the chief said to me: "Reporters last." I thought he was kidding. He wasn't.

After I got safely on the ladder, I took one last picture. It showed a gaping hole where we were standing just moments previously.

On How and How Not to Quit

There' are lots of different ways to leave a job. I've quit on the spot, been fired and left other times with zero notice. The worst way I ever did it was trying to use the "nice" method. Big mistake.

I told my boss, the publisher of the Omak Chronicle, that the time had come for me to be moving on. My wife, I explained, had grown tired of the small town and wanted out and I had reluctantly agreed.

Not wanting to leave my boss, Bruce, in a lurch, I told him I was going to start looking for a new job thereby giving him ample opportunity to find a replacement for me. He appreciated the gesture.

The problem arose when he found my replacement was ready, willing and able to start almost immediately.

He told me so and then began asking, almost daily: "Found anything yet?" And "Any prospects?" Or "How's the job hunting coming?"

He was half joking, but I started to feel pressured and ended up taking a job I really didn't want. I should have stuck to the formal two-week notice, something I now realize I have never done.

That Omak experience landed me in Lebanon, Ore., where I opened a checking account in the same bank that the newspaper used for cutting its paychecks.

Every payday, when I went in to deposit my check and

keep out a little cash, the teller would get a strange look. She'd shake her head a little, go back and look at some kind of official records, call in a management-type person for a brief conference and then, reluctantly it seemed, complete the transaction.

I didn't care for either my job, the town or these shaky finances and decided to move on after just a few weeks. Being in doubt as to the solvency of the operation I was with, I decided to be sly about it. Payday was Friday. After work Thursday, I rented a small U-Haul trailer and concealed it the best I could in my driveway.

In the dark, I loaded up the few possessions we had. In the morning, I walked the short distance to work and got my paycheck. I cashed it at the bank and closed out my account and then returned to the office to tell the boss I was finished.

He asked if I could give him more than two weeks notice. I told him I was giving him, by my calculations, a two-minute notice. He said he understood. He was nice about it. We shook hands.

I left town, unemployed with no prospects but greatly relieved.

After job interviews at the Providence Journal and the newspaper in Skowhegan, Maine, I ended up a while later working as the editor of the Sierra Vista Herald-Dispatch. Sierra Vista is in Cochise County, Arizona, close to the Mexican border and the famous old town of Tombstone.

I found myself working staggering hours to put out the semi-weekly paper. As with most small town newspapers, we had no wire services. I covered school board meetings,

City Council meetings, planning and zoning meetings and everything else except school sports. I'd leave the night meetings late, return to the office to write the story, get home in the wee hours of the morning and be back at work at 8 a.m.

For nearly two years I took no vacation. My third child, Jennifer, was born on press day. After making sure everything was OK, I left the hospital, sped to work and got the paper out, on time.

In covering all things political in town, I concluded early on that things were not right at City Hall. I didn't trust the mayor. My suspicions were confirmed as three separate sources in the inner sanctum fed me information over many months.

In the summer of 1972, things were heating up. I kept a large jar of TUMS in my desk drawer and ate them like candy.

I told the paper's general manager, my boss, I needed a brief respite and I left town with my young family for three days R&R in, of all places, El Paso. We happened upon a small "amusement park" down at the border operated by a Mexican family.

They had a small train that chugged around the perimeter of a grassy lot and a few other carnival rides. We were their only customers. A boy of about 12 years would run from ride to ride, operating whichever one we wanted to go on.

It was the perfect respite and I returned to Sierra Vista refreshed. I found in the mailbox a letter from my general manager telling me my services at the newspaper were no longer needed. No explanation. He enclosed a check for the week, nothing more.

I applied for unemployment benefits, which I was awarded after a hearing. My wife got a job at a restaurant, bringing home not only a check, but daily tips. I started stringing for both the Tucson daily papers, the Citizen and the Arizona Daily Star.

We were making more money than before, but we knew it couldn't last.

I applied at the Citizen and where it asked reason for leaving previous job, I put "Fired." The assistant managing editor, Mitch, was a maverick. He liked that and wanted to know the details. I told him what I knew.

He called the man who had fired me and asked for a recommendation. He was told that I was a good worker, writer, reporter, etc., etc. Then Mitch asked: "Why then did you fire him?"

Answer: "He wrote some stories that upset the powers that be."

Mitch: "Were the stories accurate?"

Answer: "Oh, yes!"

Mitch called me and wanted to know when I could start work.

I found out later that the mayor took advantage of my brief absence by having city workers and trucks pave the parking lot of his small shopping center at no cost to him. He was a major advertiser with the paper and told my boss he wanted me gone. My boss, having no journalism ethics background, agreed.

To my satisfaction, other large advertisers launched a boycott, which resulted in my boss losing his job.

After 23 years at the Citizen, it was again time to go. There was one problem. They had gotten in the habit of "honoring" a departing employee with an office party, complete with a fancy cake and awkward speeches.

I couldn't stomach that. I calculated that I had exactly two weeks of earned vacation time coming my way. Late on the appointed day, after most everyone was gone, I informed my department head and publisher.

I gave them a verbal two-week notice and then told them I'd be off for my final two weeks. They took it nicely.

That was a good way to leave.

And Mitch, the man who hired me at the Citizen? When he quit, a few years before, he left his clothes in a neat pile on the floor of the editor's office before strolling out the door.

Rubbing Elbows

I'm usually envious when I read the retirement stories and memoirs of the men and women of journalism.

What an exciting career it must be! Look at the travel, the thrills, the famous people they mix with.

Then I realize I spent 28½ years in that racket and none of that glamorous stuff happened to me. Where did I go wrong?

The closest I ever got to possibly being involved with a big time story came when the rumors spread that Muhammad Ali might be coming to fight in my tiny Washington town of Omak, population 4,000.

Ali was banned from boxing in the United States at the time and had been stripped of his title because he refused to be drafted into the armed forces.

A boxing promoter had a brainstorm. Because Indian reservations were their own nations, he reasoned, Ali could fight on one of those and get around the ban. Omak was actively mentioned because it had a large rodeo arena, which sat across the Okanogan River on the Colville Indian Reservation.

Alas, it never came to be. What a hoot that would have been for Omak, which billed itself as the largest city in 50,000 square miles. Talk about remote!

Then there was Dave Thomas, the founder of Wendy's, who was well-known because of all the TV spots he did for his fast-food franchise. He stopped in Tucson to inspect one of his new restaurants on Speedway Boulevard and I was dispatched to interview him.

I was the only newsman there. As we walked through the kitchen, Thomas said: "Don't ask me why I make my hamburgers square. Ask me something different."

"OK," I replied. "Why don't you make square buns?" He didn't smile.

He ordered a bowl of chili and a chicken sandwich and we sat down for lunch, just the two of us. I found out he wanted me to interview him about his pet project, adoption, which I did, gladly. I'll never forget the double-takes as customers walked through the door and saw who was sitting there, having lunch. A few took pictures (of Dave).

On another occasion, I was sent out to the University Medical Center for a story on some actor I had never heard about: Jeff Bridges. I knew of his dad, Lloyd, of course, and had heard of a son Beau. But not Jeff, although he was an established actor by that time, which was about 1990. I've never been much of a movie-goer.

Jeff was there to visit the sick kids, the really sick ones, and I was to tag along. This was no photo-op. I was the only newsman there and I didn't have a camera. He spent hours visiting children and parents. This was not the stereotype I had expected. He even donned surgical garb so he could watch part of an operation. He brightened the day for a lot of people.

When we stepped off an elevator together, a passerby did a double-take and asked: "Are you Jeff Bridges?" Hmmm, I said to myself. Maybe he's better known than I thought.

Equally surprising was Joan Embery, who made close to 100 appearances on the Johnny Carson show with a vast menagerie of wildlife specimens.

She was getting ready to go inside to address a large gathering at the Old Tucson Movie Studio when I caught her in the parking lot to to ask just a couple of quick questions for a story.

She treated me as if I was the most important person in the world and insisted on showing me some of the animals she had with her. She obviously had a passion for her calling and made sure I had every bit of information needed. I was getting uneasy at the end because it was past time for her talk to begin and the old Tucson execs were pacing nervously.

Another time, there was a large aerospace company in the Phoenix area that was proud of a state-of-the-art flight simulator it had developed to train Air Force pilots. It wanted some publicity and had invited Senator Barry Goldwater to put the simulator through its paces.

After Barry watched a couple of young active duty pilots show their stuff, he took to the full-size cockpit. Barry, by the way, was a World war II pilot who rose to the rank of major general in the air force reserve.

His mission was to attack an enemy anti-aircraft position and he did so with relish and fervor. Once on the target Barry fired missiles and machine guns and kept blasting away and away. So much so that he kept running out of ammo. But he never knew that as the folks in charge wisely kept pushing buttons to keep the senator armed.

After Barry flew, I got to do the same with a trainer at my

side as a guide. At one point I accidentally veered off course and found out the structure I was firing on was a school building. I was grounded.

The good people at Fort Huachuca once had me down to sample field rations (now known as MREs as in Meals Ready to Eat), run me through a gas chamber, have me rappel down a cliff and, as a reward, fire a couple hundred runs with an M16.

Another memorable day was a long trek on horseback with a two former World War II airmen into the Galiuro Mountains north of Willcox. That's where their WWII training flight had crashed after takeoff from Tucson.

They were among the survivors who were rescued by a local cowboy, who had seen the nighttime explosion and rode up on horseback the next day. It was a reunion between the airmen and the cowboy and the goal was to reach the crash site. Darkness cut us short and we didn't make it. But what a great way to spend a day and get paid for it.

A day in Tombstone, was memorable as well. I was there at the invitation of resident historian Ben Traywick. Terry "Ike" Clanton was in town to promote his tape: "Wyatt Earp Murdered My Cousin."

Terry got dressed up in 1880s-period clothes and wanted me to take a picture of him in a way that would show his resemblance to his fourth-generation cousin, the Ike Clanton of OK Corral infamy. I gladly complied. The resemblance was uncanny.

Then Clanton and I went over to the boardwalk outside the Crystal Palace Saloon, where Traywick was visiting with a young man, also dressed up in 1880s garb.

It turned out he was Glen Wyatt Earp, a struggling actor and fifth cousin to Wyatt. He just happened to be in town for a promo.

So there we were outside the Crystal Palace, which looks the same as it did in the 1880s. Mr. Earp, a strikingly tall, square-jawed specimen, and Mr. Clanton, a rather diminutive, squinty-eyed sort. Eerie.

Supply and Demand II

There was a previous chapter devoted to supply and demand. This is Supply and Demand II. (The "II" means I am a slow learner in some things.)

In 1988, at the age of 44, I took up oil painting as a hobby. Took lessons from Alan Smith, a bona fide professional artist, who was good at all kinds of things except naming his school. To this day I have to put on my art resumé that I studied at Alan's Art School. Couldn't he have made up something with a little more class?

Or why couldn't he have been named Alan Guggenheim? Knowing him as well as I do (he was best man at my wedding in 1996), he still would have called it Alan's Art School. I guess I should be thankful that he didn't go by Al. Or Smitty.

Anyhow, with a lot of practice and thanks to Alan Smith at Alan's Art School, I learned to paint, among other things, nice little Arizona sunsets. Painting fast, which was Alan's mantra, I could get a small painting done in 20 minutes or less.

So, I reasoned: Pop those suckers in a frame (hecho en Mexico) and even with a store-bought canvas, I'm into each one for a mere $15. Take 'em to a weekend art festival and sell them for $25.

Let's see. A $10 profit per painting. I can do three paintings per hour. $10x3 = $30 per hour. Who needs a regular paycheck?

Fortunately, I didn't quit my day job, as they say, before trying out my theory.

First stop, Sierra Vista, a nice southern Arizona town with an Army fort and an annual Arts in the Park show. Having paid my show fees and having set up my newly purchased canopy and display panels, I leaned back, nonchalant-like, and waited for the money to roll in.

Do you know how many people want a sunset painting to hang on their walls? In Sierra Vista, I can tell you, there were none that I could find that particular year. Or the next year, for that matter.

I did find one person in Kingman, another in Sonoita and another one or two somewhere along the road.

But enough with the theory of supply and demand. Economics is (are?) boring. Let's move on to art and romance.

It started with youngest daughter Jennifer announcing that she wanted her wedding in Tucson to be at La Paloma. That translates into English roughly as "Big Bucks."

That's where I got the idea of trying to sell some of my paintings at various art festivals. I had about seven years of accumulated paintings occupying space in my townhouse. Hence the Sierra Vista show.

Flush with my success there, (although I didn't sell a painting, I did sell a $2 plastic easel that held one of my paintings), I applied for a Memorial Day show up in the mountains at Greer.

A memorable show it was. It snowed. A lot. And then the wind blew. Hard. And then it got really cold. Did I mention this was an outdoor show?

But that's not why it was memorable.

Somehow, in the cold and wind, I sold a lot of paintings. I actually made a little money. But that's not why it was memorable.

One of my customers mentioned in the midst of our conversation that two of her long-time lady friends from Tucson were visiting for the weekend and would I care to stop by her cabin after the show for a beer? I apparently looked like a beer drinker. I guess it shows.

This is the memorable part. That customer was Janet. She and her friends and I sat by a roaring fire and shared a beer or two at her cozy cabin before walking on over for steaks at historic Molly Butler Lodge.

In short order, I did quit my day job of 23 years, moved to Greer, and Janet and I got hitched at the Triangle T Guest ranch in Dragoon in front of Jimmy Judd, retired Cochise County Sheriff.

Besides paying Jimmy for his services, I gave him a neat little gift: A genuine, one-of-a-kind, original, hand-crafted Peter Pegnam oil painting – of an Arizona sunset.

Understanding Banks – Sorta

You know when I realized the banks in this country were in big trouble?

The very day this Arizona-based bank in Pinetop approved a loan to refinance our property. It was back in the 1990s.

The loan seemed iffy from the start. Well, it seemed iffy to me. Not to my wife, Janet, nor to the very helpful banker in Pinetop. Both ladies were, and still are, blessed with an abundance of the can-do spirit.

The property in question consisted of three aging buildings on a half-acre of land in our remote and beautiful mountain resort town of Greer, high up in Arizona's White Mountains.

The first hurdle was an appraisal, which came in, just barely, at the minimum needed.

Hurdle No. 2 was the fact that one of the three structures was a commercial building, which housed our small real estate office and our modest (which is to say, struggling) antique business and art gallery. This was to be a residential loan. No commercial buildings allowed.

No problem, said the helpful banker. We'll just split that building off. Kinda pretend it's not there. She needed a survey map for her file showing that the loan would be on an odd-shaped parcel of land that contained but two buildings.

I paced things off and drew up the map myself. I'm not a

114

surveyor, but I can pace things off very well owing to a stride that is exactly 36 inches. Presto, one building gone.

But now things got sticky. It was touch-and-go as to our income being enough to justify the loan.

Income tax returns and financial statements were brought into play.

Part of our income was based on the fact that the two remaining structures on the property were used for nightly rentals. This was, after all, a resort town, and furnished cabins fetched a pretty price by the night. That's easy to understand when you appreciate that summer temperatures in Greer hover in the 60s when it may be 110 degrees or hotter down in the valley, also known as Phoenix.

But we harbored secret plans to stop renting out one of the buildings. It's not important to go into all the details, but suffice to say our income was going to take a hit.

Janet, being honest, felt compelled to tell the banker. I, on the other hand, made a compelling (I thought) argument for keeping mum.

"Whatever you do," I remember saying, "please, please don't tell the banker. We'll never get approved for the loan if she knows our income will be going down."

Sometime during the next couple of weeks, business brought us to Pinetop and Janet thought we should stop in at the bank and see how the loan application was coming along.

When the banker saw us coming, I caught something in her eyes I didn't like.

After a few comments on the weather, we turned to the loan.

"Before we go any further," Janet blurted out, "I need to tell you that we are going to stop renting the Homestead."

The Homestead, that's what we called the cabin in question.

I wasn't surprised by Janet telling her this. That's the way she is. Honest. To a fault, if that's possible.

What did surprise me was the banker's reaction. Her expression totally changed. Her face relaxed. She smiled, a big, genuine smile.

"Oh, that's great," she said. "I was just working on your loan and there wasn't enough income, but now there is!"

Huh? How's that? Come again.

In actuality, I stood there mum. I have learned to be quiet at times like these. Just an occasional nod of the head, as if I understand.

The explanation, I learned later, was something I have come to call accountant-think or banker-think (the latter being an apparent contradiction in terms).

Our accountant, a CPA and above-board in all her dealings, showed our rental property operating at a loss. The expenses – the principal and interest payments, taxes, insurance, gas, electric, firewood, maintenance, depreciation, etc. – all added up to less than our rental income.

As long as we were claiming that income on our loan application, we also had to claim the losses. But take away the income, see, and away go the losses.

So, by making less, we made more. Simple, huh?

But to me there was a catch. While we were in fact taking away the income, we were not eliminating the expenses. The losses would still be there. Not good.

But that's something called logic, and that has no place in the world of banking.

Only a few years later, banks started going belly-up. That surprised some people, but to me it seemed, well, logical.

Business Letters

Corporate America needs to begin hiring and promoting humorists.

The Bic Pen people had one working for them back in the 1960s, but that guy or gal couldn't get a job today what with the sourpusses now running amok in our big businesses.

Consider. I had this idea a few years back to help the big grocery chain Safeway promote one of its products. They sold Tasty Nuggets in 50-pound bags labeled "dog food."

We bought it religiously for our two dogs because, well, because it was cheap, or at least cheaper than the national brands, as Safeway was wont to brag.

At the time, we lived in the tiny village of Greer in Arizona's White Mountains, up with the elk, mountain lions, bobcats, bears, bald eagles and all kinds of other critters.

Our two dogs lived outside. We kept a big bowl on the back deck filled with Tasty Nuggets. They drank mountain-fresh water by walking a short distance to the Little Colorado River and numerous springs that dotted the meadow behind our cabin.

They were survivors and not totally dependent on us for food. One time, for instance, they dragged home the hind quarter of an elk. How they had come upon this morsel will never be known.

Nor did we ever find out, thank goodness, how one of them ended up with a whole, fresh pizza (it appeared to be pepperoni), that he brought home with a look of triumph.

That was when I started noticing that they ate Tasty Nuggets when they had to, when they couldn't find anything better.

And they were generous with their food, not minding at all that every night skunks, raccoons, feral cats and God knows what else partook of this bounty.

So I took it upon myself to make note of this and write Safeway suggesting that if they labeled Tasty Nuggets as a generic "animal food," it could widen its market and increase sales.

I put a great deal of thought into this. In my opinion, it was informative as well as a tad humorous and I hoped it might brighten someone's day.

I received back a brief form letter stating blah, blah, sorry you are dissatisfied ... ways to improve our products ... appreciate feedback ... valued customers ... blah, blah and more blah.

That's it?! A crummy form letter? No repartee?

Same thing with the Healthy Choice soup company.

I sent them a long letter congratulating them on providing me with the best damn can of carrot soup I ever had. Carrots, I noted were plump and obviously picked at the peak of perfection.

I congratulated them on surprising me with a hint of chicken flavor and even a grain or two of what appeared to be rice. They obviously cared about their product.

The only question I had was: How did such a marvelous can of carrot soup end up on my grocer's shelf with a label that read "chicken and rice?"

Back came the same form letter. Boring.

Things now appear to be getting worse. Walgreen's didn't even respond to my more recent letter suggesting that they give Smedley in packaging a raise as he had perfected his art to the degree that it was now impossible to open the impenetrable plastic cases surrounding their allergy capsules.

(I confess that I later found out it was possible to open them with a heavy-duty toe-nail clipper.)

Nor did a reply come from my old friends at Safeway after a note asking how one takes the internal temperature of an asparagus spear as is recommended on one of its frozen products.

I know of someone who received a form letter back from some big company. On the back of the letter was a stick-it note left their inadvertently. The note read: Send this guy the #3 letter.

I feel better about a company that takes the effort to communicate with its customers on a more personal level. Big business in America could use fewer stuffed-shirts and more folks with a sense of humor in the complaint department, assuming that hasn't been outsourced.

I wrote to LL Bean once as part of an office gag asking if they had any outfits suitable for our office mascot, a small lizard.

Darn, if we didn't get back the nicest letter and three hand-made, custom lizard outfits. A couple of months later, we got a Christmas card and gifts and well-wishings for our lizard.

That was even better than my pal at the Bic Pen company. After I complained about their leaky pens (in the 1960s), I received in the mail a large package of, what else, Bic pens.

They leaked. Big mess. I wrote back.

My witty friend sent me three large packages of Bic pens. They leaked. Bigger mess.

I didn't write back. Now there was someone with a sense of humor.

A Desert Rat's Survival Guide

If you see a rattlesnake disappearing down a small hole in the desert, do NOT poke a stick in the hole out of curiosity to see how deep the hole is.

I tried this once – just once – and discovered three things.

- Some of those holes look deep but actually are pretty shallow.
- Rattlesnakes do not like to be poked by a stick.
- Rattlesnakes can move really fast when they are provoked.

Fortunately, once it bolted out of the hole, this snake opted to scurry for a patch of deep grass, leaving me alone to reflect on my momentary lapse of common sense.

I have read that a young male fortified by intoxicating spirits and wishing to impress a lady is a common snakebite victim. Alcohol lowers inhibitions and slows the reflexes, not a good combination when there are poisonous snakes around.

Inattentive golfers looking for lost Titleists out in the desert rough also are frequent victims.

I had no such excuse. I was old, sober, alone and several miles from the nearest golf course.

The biggest scare I ever got from a rattlesnake was from a snake that wasn't.

I was hiking through some deep grass out in the Rincon

Mountain foothills east of Tucson. It had just quit raining and I tied my cheap plastic rain jacket around my waist.

I heard an unmistakable rattle and jumped – really, really high. When I came back down I jumped again and hopped to safety.

An inspection revealed that there was no snake. The sleeve of my plastic raincoat had brushed against dry grass with some hollow pods. Cowboys have a name for this weed. They call it Panic Grass.

That's the kind of thing that happens when you forsake trails and "bushwhack," as hikers describe it.

My son, Mike, has had to endure some of my other ill-advised hiking decisions.

After making it on the trail to the top of Wasson Peak in the Tucson Mountains, we started back down. One of the first switchbacks revealed my car way, way down at the trail head. Citing the shortest distance between two points theorem from my high school geometry class, I convinced a dubious Mike it would be a whole lot quicker to head straight down the backside of the mountain. Bushwhack it.

It was dark when we reached the parking lot, much later than if we had stuck to the trail. But we suffered only superficial scratches and minor sprains.

My son was also with me when I opted to take another shortcut in the Catalina Mountains to the north of Tucson. This one went through about a half-mile of "shin dagger" country. Shin daggers are very descriptive of one particular member of the agave family. Another painful lesson learned.

I also have vowed to pay heed when the weather forecasters advise to stay indoors.

I didn't this one time, and that's how my son and I ended up huddled under a very shallow and narrow ledge in a mountain canyon during a ferocious lightning and hail storm.

After that memory had faded a bit, my son agreed to come along on a quiet Sunday to help me explore a portion of the San Pedro River just outside the historic town of Tombstone. (You think that would've given him a clue.)

I told him we would have to be alert as there were reports of quicksand in the area. Getting from Point A to B and, with any luck, back to A, required us to wade back and forth across the river and then right down the main channel for quite a distance.

We didn't discover quicksand, but did end up with really cold feet, thereby learning that long-term exposure to even cool water can lead to hypothermia.

For whatever reason, maybe he felt like I needed looking after, Mike agreed to a backpacking trip to the Chiricahua Mountains, snuggled into Arizona's remote Southeastern corner.

We had just pitched our tents and were doing a little exploring when we heard a loud scratching sound down the hill a ways and I mouthed the word "bear!"

We crept forward until we saw two very large black bears scratching a couple of trees. When they tired of that activity, they left and continued down the mountain and out of sight. A prudent person would have said: "Wow! Wasn't that great?"

What I said was: "Let's follow 'em!"

124

When we caught up with them, we watched at what I considered to be a safe distance as they chowed down on something in a clearing. One bear was oblivious to our presence; the larger one kept looking our way.

Keeping our faces to the bears, we cautiously took a few steps backwards in hopes that the bear had read the same books I had about bear behavior and understood our sign language: "We mean you no harm. We just being stupid."

After a few minutes of this, the bigger one turned toward us and took a couple of slow and deliberate steps in our direction and then swayed back and forth, staring.

That was very clear sign language. No book needed. We retreated, quickly.

Somehow, Mike and I spent four days backpacking and exploring the Grand Canyon without incident. Go figure. Although they tell it differently, my hiking trips with my daughters, Sarah and Jennifer, also were relatively benign.

But then, there's my wife Janet, who goes by Calamity Janet. Clever, huh?

Well, you're guessing right if you think this is a bad combination – Calamity Janet and I – to be discussing a hike.

Her idea to hike up to Mount Baldy, above Greer, was exceeded in poor judgment only by my decision to go along. At an elevation of 11,420 feet, Mount Baldy gets its name from the fact that the summit is above treeline.

I didn't know that at the time we started out early in the morning. I was painfully aware of it when we struggled back into the parking lot – after dark.

On another day, we set out for a *walk*. There is a short, friendly trail that follows a small creek up to Badger Pond.

When we got there, I asked if she knew where the water comes from that feeds Badger Pond.

She said Potato Springs. I said, let's go see. She said OK. This is how a walk turned into a hike.

When we got to Potato Springs, we had just entered the edge of a beautiful aspen forest flush with fall colors. I said, it's so beautiful, let's follow the trail just a little more. She said OK.

When we walked some more, I figured it was probably shorter to continue on and come back into Greer along the Little Colorado River. A loop hike. This is how a hike turned into an ordeal.

How was I to know that the top part of the boulder-strewn Little Colorado River has no trail?

We had to bushwhack it. There's that word again. I told Janet it was pay-back for the Mount Baldy thing. She did not say OK.

Let me just say that these treks and others have let me develop an easy-to-remember back-country survival tip for others: Don't hike with me.

The Fun Is in the Planning – Really

When my kids saw the movie "National Lampoon's Vacation," they thought I should have been paid royalties.

If they're going to explain that, they'll have to do it in *their* memoirs as I have almost nothing except fond memories of our family vacations.

I know the ferry trip over to Catalina Island was on the rough side, but we made it without the barf bags that virtually all the other passengers were taking advantage of. They can thank their old mariner father who told them to go up on deck, in the fresh air, and look at something in the distance.

When we disembarked, I spotted a seaplane service. I walked directly over to the booth, pushed my credit card toward the clerk and made reservations for the return trip. I believe it's the only time in my life I purchased something without inquiring about the price. (You're welcome, my children.)

The Pismo Beach trip, now, was quite the thing. I assumed that a California beach meant good swimming. It was quite the shock when I discovered that Pismo beach was pretty much deserted. And a lot colder and blustier than I expected. This is *central* California, someone explained. Ohh.

While the family huddled out of the wind onshore, I decided to take a dip, for bragging rights. I finally made it out to waist-deep water and began splashing around when I noticed I had a friend. I'm not sure what they're called, but it was blubbery, fur-covered, had flippers and seemed to appreciate the company.

Quitting the beach, we discovered a playbill announcing a local production of "Oklahoma" for the evening. Heck, we figured, we're in California. That must mean an off-Hollywood type production. Professionals.

It actually was in a small room with a make-shift stage, folding metal chairs and locals – on the stage and in the audience (except for us). Accolades followed the performance as in: "Hey, Chet, I didn't know you could sing."

During another California vacation, we were leaving Universal Studios and were scheduled next to visit LaBrea Tar Pits because I wanted the children to have an educational experience.

We were confronted at the exit by a man waving free tickets to that afternoon's taping of the Tim Conway Show. Forget the tar pits. Imagine seeing Tim Conway AND Harvey Korman on the same stage. For free, too. Culture.

Other years I found myself explaining to the children how it would be much more fun to take an (inexpensive) Arizona holiday than the same old (expensive) trip to, say, Disneyland, SeaWorld, Knott's Berry Farm, La Jolla beaches and so on. Been there. Done that. Boring.

I am blessed with three wonderful children who always pretended to agree.

That's what brought us one year to a close call during a camping trip into the Chiricahua Mountains in southeast Arizona. The only mishap on the way were the sleeping bags spilling from the roof rack onto Interstate 10 outside of Benson.

I also miscalculated the weather. It was cold and we weren't totally prepared. After the first bone-chilling night, I was ready to leave, but was outnumbered. My eldest, Sarah, spoke for the rest when she pretty much said they were staying, with or without me. Makes a dad proud.

Later that day we were hiking on a narrow trail through the Wonderland of Rocks area with Sarah in the lead, followed by Mike and then Jennifer, who suddenly leaped an astounding distance into the air, screamed "Snake!!" and landed with her feet already running.

She had nearly stepped on a rattlesnake in the middle of the trail. The snake was riled up and ready for action. We thought that maybe Sarah or Mike had inadvertently and unknowingly stepped on it or kicked it, but we'll never know. Closer examination showed it was a dark-colored rattler. Turns out it was an Arizona Black rattlesnake, not too common.

Another Arizona camping trip took us to a remote area of the White Mountains. After freeing the car from a muddy spot on a rarely traveled back road, we found an area that looked like a good place to spend the night.

This was in the days when you could pretty much drive anywhere off-road in the National Forests. So I pointed the station wagon across an open field to a spot with trees.

We expected to hear elk bugling in the middle of the night, but didn't. We heard other animals.

On leaving the tent in the morning, we discovered that I had parked in open range country and we were in the midst of a huge herd of cattle.

This had Sarah running from tree to tree, for protection from the steers, which sported some pretty long horns. But Mike, who noticed they were lacking certain other accessories, tried giving his older sister some encouragement.

"It's OK, Sarah," he shouted across the pasture. "They're not bulls."

To which Sarah retorted: "I'm not afraid of being raped! I'm afraid of being gored!"

Hodgepodge

One spring morning in 1965, I got dressed up in a suit jacket and tie, as was expected in those days, and headed for Seattle's Sea-Tac Airport for a Northwest Orient flight to Providence, RI.

At the terminal, the airline had arranged a scrumptious breakfast buffet for passengers waiting to board.

The first leg of the flight was to Chicago. Somewhere in between the stewardesses (not flight attendants) served lunch. It was a steak (yes, steak) dinner with small boiled potatoes and other goodies.

Some passengers got off in Chicago. I was one of a few who stayed on for the next leg of the trip to New York. Once the new passengers got on and we took off again, the stewardesses served us all another meal.

Wouldn't you know it. Steak again. I was new to flying, this being my second cross-country journey, but I was beginning to like it.

I changed planes in New York for the short hop to Providence. There wasn't time for another steak dinner. But the stewardesses did bring everyone sack lunches and cold drinks.

*

My Cub Scout career lasted one day. My first-ever meeting consisted of plant identification in the Den Mother's backyard. Talk about excitement. I never went back.

A Linotype operator at the Omak Chronicle insisted on changing the word inoculation (correct spelling) in my regular measles clinic stories to innoculation (wrong spelling). She looked it up in the dictionary after I suggested to her that she might be wrong. To no avail. She continued to change it.

Diplomat (coward) that I am, I solved the dilemma by thereafter telling parents where they could bring their kids in for measles shots.

*

There's nothing like a Baby Book to make you feel old.

Inside mine is the hospital statement for my birth, Bill #176, from South County Hospital, Wakefield, R.I.. The cost of the hospital room was $6 per day. The Delivery Room charge was $15. Laboratory fees were $2 and Special Medicines came to $1.26.

Because there were complications, my mother spent eight days in the hospital, ringing up $48 in room fees.

Thus, the total charge for my birth at South County Hospital in April 1944, because of the extended stay, came to $66.26. I calculate that amounted to have been about 60 hours of pay for my father.

My first two children were born, in 1968 and 1970, at Mid-Valley Hospital in Omak, I did not have any health insurance. In fact, I don't recall knowing that any such thing existed. I paid the hospital bill and doctor over a period of time.

I don't remember that paying the doctor and hospital was a financial hardship.

In 1971, when my third child was born, in the Sierra Vista Community Hospital, I still had no insurance but did have an actual credit card. I have no idea how I qualified for the card, but I remember charging the birth. I think it was a tad under $300. I was making $170 a week, so this cost me, as with my previous examples, about 60 hours of pay.

Just a few years back, I stepped on a rusty nail and went to the clinic in Round Valley, AZ, for a tetanus shot.

I told the receptionist I did not have insurance, did not need to see a doctor and desired only a tetanus shot.

A short while later, a lady in a white uniform came out and lead me down a hallway where she gave me a shot outside a closet. The bill was less than $20.

Affordable medical care? Get the government and insurance companies out of it. My two cents worth.

*

Speaking of the government, we used sawdust heat in the 1960s to keep our old house in Omak cozy, even when temperatures dipped to 20 below zero and a hard wind pushed the chill factor to 60 below.

These were not pellets made from sawdust. This was the raw product, delivered straight from the Biles-Coleman Lumber Company. It cost $11 for a big truck load.

The truck dumped its load into a sawdust bin in the basement. I used a large metal bucket to pour the sawdust into a big hopper that fed the fire.

One winter I got lucky and was able to sneak by with just two loads – $22 to heat the house.

Of course, that was before the EPA came into existence and took care of that kind of nonsense.

133

Our phone number in Wickford when I was a kid was 906. That's what you said after the operator said "Operator." There were times my mother thought the operator stayed on the line to eavesdrop after putting a call through. Imagine that!

There were times when this snoopiness came in handy. Once when Mom tried calling Dr. Henry, our family physician, the operator told her Dr. Henry was not in the office that particular day because he was down at South County Hospital delivering so-and-so's baby.

Whenever the fire siren sounded, Dad would run to the phone and ask the operator where the fire was. She always knew, of course, and was glad to share the news.

*

I never knew the back door to our house on Pleasant Street in Wickford to be locked. We may not even have had a key.

We had a breadman, Bob Cushman, who gave the back door one knock before coming in. When there was no one home, which was often, he'd check our bread box and determine how much we needed, bread-wise. But he carried other goodies as well and might decide we needed a dozen doughnuts or a sweet roll, for example.

This led to some friendly bantering when he'd catch Mom home. She'd give him a hard time, half in jest, about leaving too many sweets just because he needed the money. He would reply that he felt we were working too hard and needed a reward or that he knew we were having company. He was our breadman for many, many years.

Our milk was delivered the same way by the Whiting Company. The milkman would decide how many quarts of milk we needed and leave it in the refrigerator (or icebox as most people still called it). After a while, he also started carrying ice cream. He would decide when we needed ice cream, not often enough for us kids but too often according to Mom.

Our mailman for many years was Frank Bordeau. He had a walking route and carried a large leather bag. During the Christmas card season, he'd walk his route twice a day.

*

Having come from a small town, Omak, Washington, seemed normal after attending Seattle University and getting a taste of city life.

My (now divorced) wife being from Spokane had difficulty adapting, especially to what she viewed as a certain nosiness. This wasn't helped by one of her first visits to Gene's IGA, where she met a lady member of the City Council who said: "I've talked so much about you. It's good to finally have a chance to meet."

Twenty-three years in Tucson got me used to the city life. Then, after meeting Janet, I moved to Greer, which sported about 90 year-round inhabitants. Now that's small!

And guess what? Janet never locked her back door. Taking it one step further, she also left the keys in the car's ignition.

*

In the late 1990s, Janet and I discovered that someone had taken up residence on land we owned in a remote part of Pinal County. So remote, that electricity is some six miles away and may never reach our parcel. The power company told me this.

Our trespasser was using a generator for his double-wide. In spite of my pleadings and urgings, he refused to budge.

Enter Casa Grande, AZ, attorney Phillip Glenn, who we hired to take up our cause. It took years because of a crowded court calendar, but common sense finally reigned and our interloper moved on.

When the legal dust settled, I did something I don't do nearly often enough. I wrote a thank-you note.

I told Mr. Glenn how much we appreciated him and his patience and efforts and thanked him for restoring peace at our "ranch," which we lovingly called our patch of desert.

I found out some time later that Mr. Glenn had died. Shocked, I called his law partner who told me that Mr. Glenn dropped dead from heart failure as he was getting ready to go to work one morning.

I checked the day he died and compared it to the date of my letter. I remembered mailing it that same day I wrote it. It was the Friday before he died. He would have received my letter Monday, probably. Tuesday at the latest. He died Wednesday.

I hope he read it and appreciated that it came from the heart.

Sorry to say, though, that there have been many, many more thank-you notes I should have written and didn't.